The Revolution Of AI Agents: How Autonomous Systems Are Transforming Technology, Business, and Society

Jayant Deshmukh

Published by Jayant Deshmukh, 2025.

Table of Contents

Disclaimer

The information provided in this book is for general informational and educational purposes only. Every effort has been made to ensure the accuracy and reliability of the content at the time of publication. However, the author and publisher make no representations or warranties regarding the completeness, accuracy, or suitability of the information contained in this book.

The tools, applications, and techniques mentioned are subject to changes in availability, pricing, and functionality by their respective developers or organizations. Readers are advised to conduct their own research and exercise discretion before using any tool or implementing any recommendations.

The author and publisher shall not be held liable for any damages, losses, or adverse consequences arising from the use or misuse of the information provided herein. Any reliance you place on the information in this book is strictly at your own risk.

This book includes references to third-party tools, websites, and applications, which are used solely for informational purposes. The inclusion of such references does not imply endorsement or affiliation with the respective developers or organizations.

THE REVOLUTION OF AI AGENTS: HOW AUTONOMOUS SYSTEMS ARE TRANSFORMING TECHNOLOGY, BUSINESS, AND SOCIETY

First edition. FEBRUARY 17, 2025.

Written by Jayant Deshmukh.

About the Author

Jayant Deshmukh is a visionary leader at the intersection of technology and human potential. Certified Project Management Professional (PMP) and an AI expert with a wealth of experience in driving digital transformation initiatives across the globe. With over 16 years in the IT industry, Jayant has had the privilege of working with numerous banks and financial institutions worldwide, helping them navigate the complexities of technological evolution and embrace the future of AI and digitalization. His expertise lies in understanding how emerging technologies, like AI, can revolutionize business models, streamline operations, and create sustainable wealth.

Jayant's professional journey has taken him to multiple countries, where he collaborated with multinational corporations (MNCs) in various sectors. This international exposure has equipped him with a deep understanding of diverse geographies, cultures, and the unique challenges faced by individuals, businesses, and societies around the world. Through his work with these corporations, he has gained valuable insights into how people, regardless of their location, share common aspirations and desires for growth, success, and financial independence. His experience allows him to design AI-driven strategies that cater to the specific needs of individuals and businesses across the globe, helping them build better lives and brighter futures.

Beyond his corporate expertise, Jayant is a thought leader in **AI, automation, and digital strategy**. His ability to bridge the gap between **technology and business impact** has made him a sought-after speaker, mentor, and consultant in the AI space.

Books Authored by Jayant Deshmukh

Jayant has penned several impactful books that reflect his expertise, passion, and vision for empowering individuals and professionals. Each book is crafted with a human touch, engaging storytelling, and actionable insights.

1. **Prompt Engineering - The Ultimate Guide for Success in Artificial Intelligence**

This definitive guide to AI prompt engineering offers a comprehensive introduction to AI interaction, helping both beginners and professionals harness AI's power. Packed with practical tools, insights, and examples, it empowers readers to leverage AI effectively in their daily and professional lives.

2. **Mastering the Art of Corporate Communication** Aimed at enhancing influence, collaboration, and leadership, this book explores 149 effective communication strategies essential for success in the corporate world. It provides actionable advice and real-life examples, equipping readers to strengthen their communication skills and make an impact in any professional setting.

3. **Step by Step Guide to Overcome Corporate Politics** Through a practical and storytelling-driven approach, this book presents 105 proven techniques to navigate and resolve corporate politics. It helps readers manage office dynamics, avoid conflicts, and thrive in their professional journeys, all while maintaining authenticity and integrity.

4. **Digital Transformation in Banking & Finance: Unlocking the Power of 110 AI Tools to Revolutionize the Banking and Finance Industry** An in-depth exploration of how AI tools are transforming the banking and finance sectors, this book provides insights into 110 AI-powered tools that enhance productivity, improve customer experiences, and drive innovation. It's a must-read for financial professionals looking to embrace AI.

5. **Building a Career in AI: A Practical Guide for Aspiring Professionals** A motivational and inspiring guide for individuals starting or transitioning into AI careers. This book offers real-life examples, practical advice, and actionable steps, serving as a roadmap for aspiring AI professionals to succeed in this dynamic field.

6. **AI Tools for Everyone: 119 Best AI Tools to Master Everyday Tasks** This book introduces readers to 119 AI tools designed to improve efficiency and productivity in everyday tasks. From personal use to business applications, Jayant demonstrates how these tools simplify processes and help users accomplish more in less time, making AI accessible to all.

7. **10x Productivity Hacks: Unlocking the Secrets of AI to Boost Productivity, Efficiency and Transform Your Life** A practical guide that shares powerful strategies and tools to dramatically enhance productivity. It offers actionable insights for individuals looking to maximize their output while maintaining a healthy work-life balance.

6

8. **Nurturing Growth Mindset: A Parent's Guide for Raising Innovative, Adaptive and Empowered Children** This book is a heartfelt guide for parents, blending Jayant's professional acumen with his personal experiences as a parent. It offers insights into equipping children with the skills, resilience, and mindset needed to thrive in the AI-driven world.

9. **AI Revolution in Medicine & HealthCare: Digital Transformation through Artificial Intelligence**

An in-depth exploration of how AI is revolutionizing the Medicine and HealthCare sector, this book is must-read for healthcare professionals looking to embrace AI.

10. **Artificial Intelligence for Financial Freedom: 100 Passive Income Strategies to Build Wealth in the Digital Era**

To harness the power of AI to create sustainable passive income streams and achieve financial independence in today's digital-first world.

11. **Future of Digital Marketing: Harnessing AI, Social Media, and Data-Driven Strategies for Personal & Professional Growth**

It explores how AI, automation, and cutting-edge digital marketing strategies are transforming businesses, empowering professionals, and shaping the future of marketing in the digital age.

In *The Revolution Of AI Agents: How Autonomous Systems Are Transforming Technology, Business, And Society* this book, explores the rapidly evolving world of **AI agents and autonomous systems**, offering insights into how businesses and individuals can **adapt, innovate, and thrive in the AI-driven future.**

Jayant's work is **not just about technology—it's about empowerment.** He believes in **making AI accessible** to businesses, professionals, and aspiring innovators, ensuring they are well-equipped to **embrace the future of AI** with confidence.

Connect with Jayant Deshmukh on social media at :

https://www.instagram.com/jayantdeshmukhofficial/

https://www.linkedin.com/in/jayant-deshmukh-pmp/

https://www.facebook.com/jayantdeshmukh01

https://www.youtube.com/@jayantdeshm

https://www.threads.net/@jayantdeshmukhofficial

https://x.com/jayantdeshm

Prologue

Every great technological shift in human history has been met with curiosity, excitement, and a fair share of skepticism. From the invention of the wheel to the rise of the internet, each breakthrough has redefined how we live, work, and interact. Today, we stand at the threshold of another transformative era—one where artificial intelligence (AI) agents are no longer science fiction but a reality shaping our world in profound ways.

I remember when I first encountered AI in its early stages—clunky, limited, and far from autonomous. It was exciting yet frustrating, promising yet constrained. Back then, AI systems were just glorified calculators, capable of following pre-set rules but incapable of real intelligence. Fast forward to today, and AI agents have evolved into sophisticated, self-learning systems that can communicate, make decisions, and even predict future outcomes.

This book is not just about AI—it is about **the revolution of AI agents** and their impact on businesses, individuals, and society as a whole. If you've ever wondered how AI is transforming industries, automating workflows, and reshaping the job market, then this book is for you. If you're an entrepreneur, a working professional, a student, or simply an enthusiast looking to understand how AI agents can be leveraged for growth, innovation, and efficiency—this book is your guide to the future.

A Brief Look at the History of AI and the Rise of AI Agents

To truly appreciate the power of AI agents, we must first understand how we got here. The concept of artificial intelligence dates back to the mid-20th century when pioneers like Alan Turing and John McCarthy laid the foundation for machine intelligence. The first few decades of AI research were filled with ambitious goals but were often hampered by the limitations of computing power and data availability.

Then came the 21st century—the golden age of AI. With the explosion of big data, advancements in deep learning, and the rise of cloud computing, AI finally had the resources it needed to flourish. Technologies like machine learning, natural language processing (NLP), and neural networks gave birth to **AI agents**—autonomous digital assistants that could understand, learn, and act on behalf of humans.

These AI agents started as simple chatbots answering customer queries but quickly evolved into sophisticated systems capable of managing complex business operations, writing software code, automating financial decisions, and even diagnosing medical conditions. Today, AI agents are present in every industry—healthcare, finance, marketing, e-commerce, supply chain, cybersecurity, and beyond.

The Current Landscape: How AI Agents Are Redefining Work and Business

Take a moment to reflect on how much the world has changed in just the past decade. A few years ago, automation was limited to routine, rule-based tasks. But now, AI agents are performing **creative, strategic, and even decision-making roles** that were once reserved for human experts.

Imagine this:

- A startup founder wants to build a software product but has no programming experience. AI-powered coding assistants like **GitHub Copilot** or **CodeWhisperer** help them write functional code.

- A marketing team needs to create personalized customer interactions at scale. AI-driven automation tools like **ChatGPT, Google Gemini, or Jasper AI** generate high-quality content, respond to customer inquiries, and optimize campaigns.
- A financial analyst needs to predict market trends. AI-powered decision-making systems analyze vast amounts of data and provide **real-time insights**, reducing the risk of human error.

These are not futuristic scenarios. They are happening **right now**, and businesses that are not adapting are already falling behind. The world is not waiting—AI agents are already embedded in the tools we use daily, from email filtering and smart assistants to complex enterprise systems managing millions of transactions.

How Businesses and Individuals Can Adapt and Thrive

With such rapid advancements, the pressing question is: **What should businesses and individuals do to keep up?**

1. Adopt an AI-First Mindset

The first step in embracing the AI agent revolution is changing the way we think about AI. It is no longer just an add-on feature or a luxury; it is a necessity. **Businesses that fail to integrate AI-driven automation risk becoming obsolete.**

Whether you're a solopreneur or a Fortune 500 CEO, you need to assess how AI can streamline your operations, improve customer experiences, and enhance decision-making. **AI is not replacing humans—it is augmenting human capabilities.**

2. Invest in AI Skills and Reskilling Programs

The workforce is evolving. While AI automates many tasks, it also creates new opportunities. The demand for AI-related skills—such as **prompt engineering, AI governance, automation strategy, and data literacy**—is skyrocketing.

Individuals must invest in learning **how to work alongside AI** rather than fear its advancements. Businesses, on the other hand, must take proactive steps in **reskilling their workforce** so that employees can transition into more strategic roles that leverage AI rather than compete against it.

3. Leverage No-Code and Low-Code AI Solutions

One of the biggest barriers to AI adoption used to be **technical complexity**. But that is changing with the rise of **no-code and low-code AI platforms**.

Tools like **Zapier, Make (Integromat), and n8n** allow businesses to **automate complex workflows** without needing deep coding expertise. AI-powered website builders, chatbot creators, and workflow automation tools empower even **non-technical users** to harness AI's potential.

The message here is simple: **AI is no longer reserved for tech giants. Anyone can build and deploy AI-powered systems.**

4. Focus on Responsible AI and Ethical Considerations

With great power comes great responsibility. The rise of AI agents has also sparked concerns over **data privacy, bias, and ethical AI governance**. Businesses must ensure that the AI systems they deploy are **transparent, fair, and free from unintended biases**.

This means implementing **AI governance frameworks**, ensuring AI systems are **explainable**, and taking proactive measures to **avoid**

discrimination or **unfair** **decision-making** in AI-powered applications.

5. Experiment, Innovate, and Stay Ahead of the Curve

The best way to prepare for the AI-driven future is to **actively experiment** with AI technologies. **Try AI-powered automation tools in your workflow, explore AI-driven decision-making platforms, and encourage innovation within your organization.**

Companies like Amazon, Tesla, and Google are not waiting for AI to become mainstream; they are **shaping the AI revolution.** The same applies to individuals—those who **embrace AI and experiment with it today will be the leaders of tomorrow.**

The Path Forward: A Future Powered by AI Agents

We are entering an era where **AI agents will be as common as smartphones**—an invisible yet powerful force driving efficiency, innovation, and growth. Businesses that adopt AI-driven automation will **outperform** their competitors, and individuals who integrate AI into their skill sets will **future-proof their careers.**

But the AI agent revolution is not just about efficiency—it is about **unlocking human potential.** Imagine a world where AI takes care of mundane, repetitive tasks, allowing us to focus on **creativity, problem-solving, and meaningful human interactions.**

The question is no longer **"Will AI agents shape the future?"**—they already are. The real question is, **"Are you ready to be a part of this revolution?"**

This book will serve as your roadmap to understanding, adapting to, and leveraging AI agents for success. Whether you are an entrepreneur looking to scale your business, a professional aiming to stay relevant, or simply an enthusiast curious about what's next—**this journey is just beginning.**

Let's embrace the AI agent revolution together. ◈

Introduction

My Journey into AI-Driven Digital Transformation

I still remember the first time I saw AI in action. It wasn't a sci-fi moment with humanoid robots or sentient machines—it was something far simpler, yet far more profound. Years ago, while working with a leading bank on digital transformation, we faced a challenge: how to process thousands of customer requests efficiently, without compromising on personalization.

Our team experimented with an AI-powered chatbot, one of the earliest conversational AI models. It was clunky at first, making mistakes that often left customers frustrated. But as we iterated and refined it, something incredible happened. The chatbot started understanding nuances, resolving queries in seconds, and even predicting customer needs before they explicitly asked. That was the moment I realized AI wasn't just about automation; it was about augmentation—enhancing human capabilities, making businesses smarter, and transforming industries.

Fast forward to today, and we stand on the brink of an AI revolution driven by autonomous agents. These are not just chatbots or rule-based automation systems; they are **self-learning, self-operating AI entities that can think, act, and make decisions in real time.** From managing complex workflows to writing software code and even running businesses, AI agents are reshaping the way we work, innovate, and interact with technology.

In this book, we will dive deep into this revolution, exploring how **AI agents, no-code/low-code AI tools, and autonomous software**

development are unlocking new possibilities. But before we get there, let's break it down step by step.

What Are AI Agents & Why Do They Matter?

To put it simply, **AI agents are intelligent systems that can perform tasks autonomously, learn from data, and interact with their environment without human intervention.** They are designed to **sense, analyze, act, and improve over time.**

Think of AI agents as digital employees, but with superpowers. Unlike traditional automation tools that rely on predefined rules, AI agents have the ability to:

- **Understand natural language** (like ChatGPT or Google Gemini)
- **Make intelligent decisions** (like an AI-powered stock trading system)
- **Automate workflows** (like UiPath, Zapier, or Make)
- **Develop software autonomously** (like OpenAI Codex, AutoGPT, and Tabnine)
- **Manage business operations** (like AI-driven customer support and AI marketing automation tools)

The Growing Impact of AI Agents on Businesses & Society

The impact of AI agents is already visible across industries:

- **Finance:** AI-powered trading bots execute trades in milliseconds, analyzing market trends better than any human trader.
- **Healthcare:** AI agents assist doctors by diagnosing diseases with greater accuracy than ever before.
- **E-commerce:** AI recommendation engines personalize

shopping experiences, increasing conversion rates and customer satisfaction.

- **Customer Service:** Virtual AI assistants handle customer queries, reducing human workload and improving response times.

One of the most compelling examples of AI agents in action is **AutoGPT**—an autonomous AI that can break down a complex goal, find relevant data, and execute tasks independently. Imagine an AI agent that can not only write software code but also debug it, test it, and deploy it—all without human intervention. That's where the future is headed.

Why AI Agents Are the Next Big Revolution in Automation

For decades, automation has been about reducing human effort in repetitive tasks. But AI agents go far beyond that. **They don't just automate; they innovate.**

Let's take an example from software development. Traditionally, a software engineer writes code, tests it, fixes bugs, and deploys the final product. Today, AI-powered tools like **GitHub Copilot and Amazon CodeWhisperer** assist developers by suggesting code snippets. But what if an AI agent could build an entire software product by itself?

We're already seeing glimpses of this with **AutoGPT and BabyAGI**—AI models that can analyze requirements, write code, troubleshoot errors, and continuously improve their own outputs. In a few years, businesses might not need teams of developers; instead, they could rely on AI-driven DevOps agents that manage the entire software lifecycle autonomously.

The Paradigm Shift in Business & Technology

The rise of AI agents marks a paradigm shift where:

- **Businesses move from rule-based automation to intelligent decision-making systems.**
- **Software is developed not by humans alone, but through human-AI collaboration.**
- **Workflows are no longer manually designed but are dynamically optimized by AI in real-time.**
- **The workforce evolves from execution-driven roles to strategy and oversight.**

This transformation is not just an efficiency gain—it's a reinvention of **how we build technology, interact with data, and create value.**

The Role of No-Code/Low-Code AI in Democratizing AI

One of the biggest barriers to AI adoption has always been the need for technical expertise. Traditionally, AI development required deep knowledge of programming, machine learning models, and data science. But thanks to the rise of **no-code and low-code AI platforms**, that's no longer the case.

No-code/low-code AI is doing for AI what website builders did for web development. Earlier, you needed coding expertise to build a website. Today, platforms like Wix, WordPress, and Webflow allow anyone to create professional websites without writing a single line of code. **The same shift is happening in AI.**

Top No-Code/Low-Code AI Tools Enabling the AI Revolution

- **No-Code AI Tools:**
  - **Bubble** – Build AI-powered web applications with drag-and-drop features.
  - **Zapier & Make (Integromat)** – Automate workflows with AI-

powered integrations.

- ○ **Adalo** – Create mobile apps without coding.
- ○ **Peltarion** – Train and deploy AI models without writing code.
- **Low-Code AI Tools:**
  - ○ **Microsoft Power Automate** – AI-driven business process automation.
  - ○ **Google AutoML** – Build AI models with minimal coding.
  - ○ **DataRobot** – AI model development with an easy-to-use interface.
  - ○ **UiPath** – AI-powered robotic process automation (RPA).

How No-Code AI is Empowering Non-Technical Users

With these tools, entrepreneurs, marketers, and business professionals can leverage AI **without needing a PhD in machine learning.** They can create AI-powered chatbots, automate marketing campaigns, or even develop AI-driven financial models—simply by using intuitive interfaces.

This democratization of AI is a **game-changer.** It means AI is no longer confined to large tech companies; it's accessible to small businesses, startups, and even individuals looking to innovate.

The Shift Towards Intelligent, Self-Operating Systems

The end goal of AI agents is **autonomy**—systems that can learn, adapt, and improve without human intervention.

We're already seeing this happen:

- **Self-driving cars** (Tesla's Autopilot, Waymo) are AI agents making real-time driving decisions.
- **AI-powered personal assistants** (Google Assistant, Siri) are evolving from simple task execution to proactive problem-

solving.

- **Autonomous trading systems** are making financial decisions with precision and speed unmatched by humans.
- **AI-driven content creation tools** (ChatGPT, Jasper, Synthesia) are generating articles, code, and even videos autonomously.

Where Are We Headed?

As AI agents become more advanced, the possibilities are limitless. We could soon see:

- AI agents that **run entire businesses** without human oversight.
- AI-powered **digital employees** managing HR, sales, and customer service.
- **Autonomous scientific research**—AI making new discoveries in medicine, physics, and engineering.

We are standing at the threshold of a revolution. AI agents, **no-code/low-code AI platforms, and autonomous systems** are not just futuristic concepts—they are reshaping our world **right now.**

In the chapters ahead, we'll dive deeper into these transformations, exploring how businesses and individuals can harness AI to drive innovation, efficiency, and success. **The AI Agent Revolution has begun—are you ready to embrace it?**

" *The future belongs to those who embrace change, not fear it. AI agents are not here to replace us but to elevate us—to amplify our intelligence, accelerate our ambitions, and unlock possibilities beyond imagination.*"

– Jayant Deshmukh

Chapter 1: Understanding AI Agents – The New Digital Workforce

The Dawn of AI Agents: A New Era of Digital Workers

For decades, we have imagined a future where machines don't just follow our commands but think, learn, and act independently. Science fiction has long been filled with intelligent robots assisting humans, but today, this vision is no longer just fiction. AI agents, the new digital workforce, are here, transforming industries, automating processes, and redefining how businesses operate. But what exactly are AI agents, and how do they differ from bots and traditional automation? Let's embark on a journey to understand this revolutionary shift.

What Are AI Agents? The Difference Between AI Agents, Bots, and Traditional Automation

At first glance, AI agents, bots, and traditional automation might seem interchangeable. However, they are fundamentally different in their capabilities, intelligence, and autonomy.

- **Traditional Automation**: These are rule-based systems that perform repetitive tasks based on predefined instructions. Think of macros in Excel or robotic process automation (RPA) tools that automate form-filling.
- **Bots**: Bots are simple software programs designed to execute specific tasks, such as chatbots that provide canned responses or web scrapers that collect data from websites.
- **AI Agents**: Unlike bots and traditional automation, AI agents have the ability to make decisions, learn from data, and act independently. They can analyze patterns, predict outcomes, and even refine their strategies over time without human

intervention.

A great analogy is comparing these three systems to different modes of transportation. Traditional automation is like a railway train—it follows a fixed track and cannot deviate. Bots are like remote-controlled cars—they require human input to operate effectively. AI agents, however, are like autonomous self-driving cars—they analyze their surroundings, make decisions, and learn from experience to improve over time.

Types of AI Agents

AI agents are not a one-size-fits-all solution. Depending on their capabilities and intelligence levels, they can be categorized into three main types:

1. Reactive Agents (Basic Rule-Based Systems)

These are the simplest AI agents, operating based on a set of predefined rules. They react to inputs in a predictable manner but lack memory or the ability to learn from past experiences.

Example: A chess-playing AI that only reacts to the opponent's current move without considering past moves or future possibilities. It follows a set of programmed rules but doesn't adapt or evolve.

2. Predictive Agents (ML-Based Decision-Making)

Predictive agents go a step further by incorporating machine learning models. These agents analyze historical data to make informed decisions and predictions.

Example: Recommendation engines on platforms like Netflix or Amazon. These AI agents analyze past user behavior to suggest relevant content or products, improving user engagement and sales.

3. Autonomous Agents (Self-Learning & Evolving AI)

The most advanced AI agents, autonomous agents can learn, evolve, and make decisions without human intervention. They use reinforcement learning, deep learning, and neural networks to adapt over time.

Example: Self-driving cars or AI-powered trading systems in financial markets that continuously analyze real-time data, adjust their strategies, and optimize performance autonomously.

The History and Evolution of AI Agents

To appreciate the significance of AI agents, let's take a look at how they have evolved over the years:

- **1950s – The Birth of AI:** Alan Turing's work laid the foundation for artificial intelligence, with early AI models focusing on basic problem-solving.
- **1980s – Expert Systems:** AI saw a rise in rule-based expert systems that mimicked human decision-making in specialized fields like medical diagnostics.
- **2000s – Machine Learning Revolution:** With the explosion of data and computing power, AI began shifting towards predictive modeling and machine learning-based decision-making.
- **2010s – The Age of Deep Learning:** Breakthroughs in deep learning enabled AI to perform complex tasks like image recognition, natural language processing, and autonomous driving.
- **2020s – The Rise of AI Agents:** Today, AI agents are at the forefront of automation, capable of learning, adapting, and making decisions in real-time.

How Businesses Are Adopting AI Agents for Growth

Businesses across industries are leveraging AI agents to improve efficiency, reduce costs, and enhance customer experiences. Here are a few real-world examples:

- **Healthcare:** AI-powered diagnostic tools like IBM Watson Health assist doctors in analyzing medical data and suggesting treatments, leading to faster and more accurate diagnoses.
- **Finance:** AI-driven trading bots analyze market trends and execute trades at lightning speed, optimizing investment strategies.
- **Customer Support:** AI chatbots handle customer inquiries, reducing wait times and improving service efficiency for companies like Amazon and Google.
- **Manufacturing:** AI agents in factories optimize supply chain operations, predict maintenance needs, and automate quality control.

The Future of AI Agents

AI agents are not just a passing trend; they are shaping the future of technology. As they become more intelligent and autonomous, they will drive the next wave of digital transformation, unlocking new possibilities in automation, innovation, and business growth.

Are you ready to embrace the AI agent revolution? The journey has just begun, and in the coming chapters, we will dive deeper into how you can leverage AI agents to transform your business and career.

Chapter 2: The No-Code/Low-Code AI Revolution

The Democratization of AI: A Revolution in the Making

Imagine a world where you don't need to be a software engineer to build AI-driven applications. A world where businesses, entrepreneurs, and even students can create sophisticated AI solutions without writing a single line of code. This is not some futuristic dream—it's happening now, thanks to the No-Code/Low-Code AI revolution.

For decades, AI development was reserved for an elite group of data scientists and programmers. Companies had to invest heavily in technical talent, making AI adoption an expensive and complex process. But today, thanks to No-Code and Low-Code platforms, the barriers are coming down. These tools empower professionals from all backgrounds—marketers, business owners, educators—to build, deploy, and scale AI solutions with minimal or no coding knowledge.

This chapter explores how No-Code/Low Code AI is revolutionizing industries, making AI accessible to a broader audience, and reshaping the future of software development.

What is No-Code/Low-Code AI, and Why is it Game-Changing?

At its core, No-Code/Low-Code AI is about accessibility and efficiency. These platforms allow users to create AI applications without extensive programming knowledge, using drag-and-drop interfaces, pre-built models, and automated workflows.

- **No-Code AI**: Eliminates the need for coding altogether. Users can design and deploy AI solutions through intuitive visual interfaces.

- **Low-Code AI**: Requires some level of coding but significantly reduces development time by providing reusable components and automation tools.

This shift is game-changing because it democratizes AI, enabling non-technical individuals and small businesses to harness AI-driven automation, data analysis, and decision-making without major investments in specialized talent.

Why is No-Code/Low-Code AI Important?

1. **Empowers Non-Technical Users** – Business professionals, analysts, and even students can create AI solutions without coding expertise.
2. **Accelerates Innovation** – Organizations can prototype and deploy AI applications rapidly, without long development cycles.
3. **Reduces Costs** – Companies no longer need large AI teams, making advanced technology accessible even to startups and small businesses.
4. **Enhances Productivity** – Automating workflows with AI can eliminate manual tasks, allowing teams to focus on strategic work.

Example: A small business owner can set up an AI-powered chatbot to handle customer service inquiries using No-Code platforms like Bubble or Adalo—without hiring a developer.

How No-Code/Low-Code AI Enables Non-Technical Users

No-Code/Low-Code AI platforms simplify the AI development process in several ways:

1. **Visual Programming Interfaces** – Users can create AI

workflows through drag-and-drop functionalities instead of writing complex algorithms.

2. **Pre-Trained AI Models** – Many platforms provide built-in machine learning models that can be customized for different use cases.

3. **Automated Integrations** – AI can be seamlessly integrated into existing business systems with minimal setup.

4. **Fast Deployment** – AI solutions can be built, tested, and deployed in days rather than months.

This accessibility allows professionals with domain expertise—such as marketers, healthcare workers, and educators—to build AI solutions tailored to their specific needs without requiring programming skills.

Example: A healthcare clinic can use No-Code AI to develop a symptom-checker chatbot that provides preliminary diagnoses to patients before they visit a doctor.

Leading Platforms for No-Code/Low-Code AI Development

Several platforms are leading the No-Code/Low-Code AI revolution. These tools empower users to build AI applications effortlessly.

No-Code AI Tools

1. **Bubble** – A visual programming tool for building AI-powered web applications.

2. **Zapier** – Automates workflows by connecting different apps and services.

3. **Adalo** – Helps users create AI-powered mobile apps without coding.

4. **Peltarion** – Provides pre-built AI models for industries like healthcare and finance.

Low-Code AI Tools

1. **Microsoft Power Automate** – AI-driven automation for businesses to streamline workflows.
2. **Google AutoML** – Allows users to train custom machine learning models with minimal coding.
3. **DataRobot** – Provides an AI platform for predictive analytics and business intelligence.

These tools allow businesses of all sizes to integrate AI into their operations without investing in large IT teams.

Case Studies: Businesses Leveraging No-Code AI Successfully

1. Healthcare: AI-Powered Diagnostics Without a Tech Team

A mid-sized healthcare clinic in Europe used **Peltarion** to build an AI-powered diagnostic tool that analyzes patient symptoms and suggests possible conditions. Within months, the clinic improved diagnosis accuracy by 30% and significantly reduced patient wait times.

2. E-Commerce: Personalized Shopping Experiences Without Developers

A fashion startup leveraged **Bubble** to develop a recommendation engine that suggests outfits based on user preferences. This AI-driven personalization increased conversion rates by 25%, enhancing customer engagement.

3. Finance: Automating Loan Approvals with Google AutoML

A microfinance institution used **Google AutoML** to build an AI-powered risk assessment model for loan approvals. The automated process reduced loan processing time from weeks to hours, improving accessibility for small businesses in need of funding.

These real-world examples illustrate how No-Code/Low-Code AI tools are revolutionizing industries by making AI accessible to everyone.

The Future of No-Code/Low-Code AI: A World of Possibilities

The No-Code/Low-Code AI revolution is only beginning. As these platforms evolve, AI will become even more accessible, enabling individuals and businesses to create intelligent solutions with unprecedented ease.

What's Next?

- **AI-Powered Personalization** – Businesses will be able to tailor customer experiences in real-time using No-Code AI.
- **Autonomous AI Systems** – AI agents will become more capable, requiring even less human intervention.
- **Industry-Specific AI Models** – Pre-trained models tailored for specific industries will drive AI adoption further.

The future belongs to those who embrace AI-driven automation, and with No-Code/Low-Code tools, that future is within reach for everyone.

Final Thoughts: Join the AI Revolution

No-Code and Low-Code AI platforms are not just technological advancements—they are enablers of creativity and innovation. Whether you're a business owner, a marketer, or an educator, AI is no longer out of reach. The power to build intelligent solutions is in your hands.

Are you ready to be part of this transformation? The No-Code/Low-Code AI revolution is here, and it's reshaping the way we work, create, and innovate.

Chapter 3: AI Tools for Building AI Agents & Automation

The Rise of AI Agent Development Tools: A New Era of Automation

Imagine walking into a store where a virtual assistant greets you, understands your preferences, and recommends products tailored to your needs. Or calling customer service and speaking to an AI that not only resolves your queries efficiently but also learns from every interaction to improve over time. These aren't futuristic concepts; they are the reality of AI agents today, and they are powered by a growing arsenal of AI development tools.

In the past, developing AI agents required extensive programming knowledge, massive computing power, and a deep understanding of machine learning algorithms. However, with the rise of No-Code/Low-Code AI and intelligent automation tools, businesses can now build and deploy AI agents with unprecedented ease.

AI agents are transforming industries—from healthcare to finance, e-commerce to logistics—by handling tasks such as customer support, data analysis, fraud detection, and workflow automation. In this chapter, we will explore some of the most powerful AI tools available today and how they enable businesses to integrate AI-driven automation seamlessly.

Key Platforms for Creating AI Agents

The world of AI agents is diverse, with different tools catering to specific functions such as conversation, automation, decision-making, and workflow management. Below, we will explore the major platforms that empower businesses to create intelligent AI agents.

1. Conversational AI: Giving AI Agents a Voice

Conversational AI has revolutionized the way businesses interact with customers. Whether it's chatbots on websites or virtual assistants on smart devices, AI-driven conversational tools provide human-like interactions that enhance customer experience.

Leading Conversational AI Tools

1. **ChatGPT (OpenAI)**
   - One of the most advanced natural language processing models, ChatGPT can engage in human-like conversations, assist with customer service, generate content, and even act as a virtual assistant.
   - **Example:** A retail company integrates ChatGPT into its website, allowing customers to receive personalized product recommendations in real-time.
2. **Google Gemini (formerly Bard)**
   - A powerful conversational AI designed for answering queries, generating content, and providing real-time information.
   - **Example:** A marketing firm uses Gemini to automate customer engagement on social media, responding to comments and queries efficiently.
3. **Amazon Lex**
   - This tool helps businesses build conversational interfaces into applications using voice and text. It's the same technology behind Amazon Alexa.
   - **Example:** A banking app integrates Amazon Lex to assist customers in checking account balances and making transactions through voice commands.
4. **IBM Watson Assistant**
   - A sophisticated AI-driven chatbot that understands

complex customer queries and provides data-driven responses.

- **Example:** A healthcare provider uses Watson Assistant to triage patient symptoms before scheduling doctor appointments.

2. Process Automation: AI-Powered Workflow Efficiency

Process automation is critical for businesses looking to improve efficiency, reduce errors, and eliminate repetitive tasks. AI-driven automation tools handle everything from data entry to invoice processing and compliance checks.

Leading Process Automation Tools

1. **UiPath**
   - A leader in robotic process automation (RPA), UiPath allows businesses to automate complex workflows with AI capabilities.
   - **Example:** A finance company automates invoice processing, reducing manual work and speeding up payments.
2. **Automation Anywhere**
   - Offers a robust platform for business process automation, integrating AI to enhance decision-making.
   - **Example:** A telecom company uses Automation Anywhere to handle customer onboarding, reducing processing time from hours to minutes.
3. **Microsoft Power Automate**
   - A Low-Code automation tool that integrates with Microsoft services to streamline workflows and enhance productivity.

- ○ **Example:** A sales team automates lead generation using Power Automate, ensuring every inquiry is tracked and followed up on without manual intervention.

3. AI-Powered RPA: The Next Level of Intelligent Automation

Traditional RPA automates rule-based tasks, but AI-powered RPA goes further by enabling systems to learn and adapt. These tools combine machine learning with automation to make intelligent decisions.

Top AI-Powered RPA Tools

1. **Blue Prism**
   - ○ A pioneer in intelligent automation, Blue Prism integrates AI and analytics to optimize business operations.
   - ○ **Example:** A logistics company uses Blue Prism to automate shipment tracking and optimize delivery routes.
2. **WorkFusion**
   - ○ Automates business processes using AI and machine learning, especially in finance and healthcare sectors.
   - ○ **Example:** A bank employs WorkFusion to detect fraudulent transactions in real-time.
3. **Pega AI**
   - ○ A robust AI-powered automation tool that assists businesses in decision-making and workflow optimization.
   - ○ **Example:** A customer service center integrates Pega AI to predict customer needs and provide personalized responses.

4. AI Decision-Making Tools: Empowering Smarter Business Choices

AI-driven decision-making tools analyze large datasets, identify patterns, and suggest optimal business strategies. These tools help businesses stay ahead of trends and make informed decisions.

Key AI Decision-Making Tools

1. **OpenAI Codex**
   - A powerful AI that helps developers write and debug code, streamlining software development.
   - **Example:** A startup leverages Codex to speed up application development, reducing coding errors and time to market.
2. **Google Vertex AI**
   - A comprehensive machine learning platform that enables businesses to build and deploy AI models with minimal effort.
   - **Example:** A retail company uses Vertex AI to analyze purchasing patterns and optimize inventory management.
3. **Meta AI**
   - Focuses on deep learning and AI research, providing tools for advanced AI applications.
   - **Example:** A media company leverages Meta AI to personalize content recommendations for its users.

How Businesses Can Integrate AI Agents Using These Tools

The successful adoption of AI agents requires a strategic approach. Here's a step-by-step guide for businesses looking to integrate AI-driven automation into their operations:

Step 1: Identify the Right Use Case

Before implementing AI, businesses must determine where AI agents can provide the most value. Common use cases include:

- **Customer support** (chatbots, voice assistants).
- **Process automation** (data entry, compliance monitoring).
- **Predictive analytics** (demand forecasting, fraud detection).

Example: A hospital identifies that scheduling patient appointments manually is time-consuming. By deploying an AI assistant, they streamline the process, reducing wait times and improving patient satisfaction.

Step 2: Choose the Right AI Tool

Once the use case is clear, businesses must select the appropriate AI tool based on functionality, scalability, and ease of integration.

Example: A marketing agency chooses ChatGPT for customer engagement and Power Automate for internal workflow automation.

Step 3: Train and Customize the AI Agent

AI agents perform best when trained on relevant data. Businesses must:

- Provide structured training datasets.
- Fine-tune models based on real-world interactions.
- Continuously update AI to improve performance.

Example: A retail company fine-tunes its chatbot to understand common customer queries specific to their products.

Step 4: Deploy and Monitor AI Performance

After deployment, businesses should:

- Track AI performance using key metrics (response time, accuracy, user satisfaction).
- Gather feedback and iterate for continuous improvement.

Example: A financial institution monitors its AI fraud detection tool to ensure accuracy and minimize false positives.

The Future of AI Agents & Automation

AI tools are evolving rapidly, making AI agents smarter, more autonomous, and deeply integrated into business processes. The future holds:

- **AI agents that self-learn and adapt without human intervention.**
- **Greater personalization in customer interactions.**
- **Seamless collaboration between AI and human workers.**

Businesses that embrace AI-driven automation today will be better positioned for the future. AI agents are not replacing human workers; they are augmenting capabilities, making work more efficient and impactful.

Final Thoughts: Embrace the AI-Driven Future

AI tools for building AI agents are no longer a luxury—they are a necessity. Whether you're a startup, a large enterprise, or an individual entrepreneur, the right AI tools can transform the way you work, engage customers, and drive innovation.

Are you ready to integrate AI into your business? The tools are here, the possibilities are endless, and the future is AI-driven. ◈

Chapter 4: AI-Powered Workflow Automation

The Transition from Manual Workflows to AI-Driven Automation

Think about the last time you performed a repetitive task—perhaps manually entering data into a spreadsheet, sending follow-up emails, or reviewing documents for errors. Now, imagine if you could automate these processes with an intelligent system that not only executes tasks flawlessly but also learns and optimizes itself over time. This is the power of AI-driven workflow automation.

In the past, businesses operated with heavily manual workflows. A retail store, for instance, would have employees handling inventory updates, managing sales records, and coordinating logistics—all prone to human error and inefficiencies. The finance sector relied on employees manually reviewing financial reports, leading to delays and inaccuracies. Even in customer service, human agents had to go through long lists of queries, responding one by one.

With AI-powered workflow automation, businesses no longer have to rely solely on human effort to manage these operations. AI systems can now handle tasks that used to take hours or days, significantly reducing costs and improving efficiency. Whether it's automating marketing campaigns, streamlining supply chain operations, or optimizing customer interactions, AI is transforming the way work gets done.

How AI Streamlines Business Processes Across Industries

AI is not just about replacing human effort; it's about enhancing efficiency, accuracy, and scalability across various industries. Let's explore how AI-driven workflow automation is revolutionizing different sectors:

1. Healthcare: Faster and More Accurate Patient Care

- **Challenge:** Hospitals and clinics deal with vast amounts of patient data, appointment scheduling, and insurance processing, often leading to delays.
- **AI Solution:** AI-powered automation tools can analyze medical records, schedule appointments, and even assist in diagnosing diseases by scanning patient history and lab results.
- **Example:** A hospital in New York implemented AI-driven scheduling software that reduced patient wait times by 30%, allowing doctors to see more patients without overburdening administrative staff.

2. Finance: Automating Compliance and Fraud Detection

- **Challenge:** Financial institutions must process large volumes of transactions while ensuring compliance with regulatory requirements.
- **AI Solution:** AI-powered workflow automation tools can flag suspicious transactions in real time and automate compliance reporting.
- **Example:** A bank integrated an AI system that automatically scans and verifies customer documents for compliance, reducing processing time from weeks to mere minutes.

3. E-commerce: Optimizing Order Fulfillment and Customer Service

- **Challenge:** Online stores struggle with handling customer orders, managing returns, and responding to customer queries efficiently.
- **AI Solution:** AI-powered automation tools help track

inventory, generate automatic order confirmations, and provide personalized customer support through AI chatbots.

- **Example:** Amazon uses AI-powered logistics automation to predict demand, ensuring that high-demand products are stocked efficiently in warehouses near customers.

4. Human Resources: Intelligent Recruitment and Employee Engagement

- **Challenge:** HR teams spend significant time sorting resumes, scheduling interviews, and onboarding new employees.
- **AI Solution:** AI tools can screen resumes, shortlist candidates based on job descriptions, and even conduct initial interviews through AI-driven chatbots.
- **Example:** A multinational corporation integrated AI into its HR process, reducing the time to hire by 50% while ensuring a fair and bias-free selection process.

5. Manufacturing & Supply Chain: Enhancing Productivity and Predictive Maintenance

- **Challenge:** Manufacturing plants require careful coordination of machinery maintenance, supplier coordination, and inventory management.
- **AI Solution:** AI-driven automation tools can predict machinery breakdowns before they occur, optimize supply chain logistics, and automate quality control.
- **Example:** Tesla's factories use AI-powered robots for assembly, ensuring higher efficiency and precision while reducing human labor in repetitive tasks.

Tools for Workflow Automation: The AI-Driven Workhorses

Businesses today have access to an array of workflow automation tools that streamline operations and integrate seamlessly with existing systems. Let's look at some of the top tools available:

1. Make (formerly Integromat)

- **What it does:** Make enables users to visually create, build, and automate workflows between different apps and services.
- **How it works:** It connects applications, allowing businesses to create multi-step workflows that trigger actions based on predefined conditions.
- **Example:** A travel agency uses Make to automatically send itinerary details to customers via email and SMS once they book a trip, eliminating manual follow-ups.

2. Zapier

- **What it does:** A popular Low-Code automation tool that connects thousands of apps and automates repetitive tasks without the need for coding.
- **How it works:** Users create "Zaps" that define triggers and actions, enabling automatic data flow between applications.
- **Example:** An e-commerce store integrates Zapier to automatically send order details from Shopify to Google Sheets, keeping inventory records updated without manual input.

3. n8n

- **What it does:** An open-source workflow automation platform that allows businesses to automate processes with complete control over data.
- **How it works:** Unlike other automation tools, n8n provides

flexibility, allowing businesses to create complex workflows tailored to their specific needs.

- **Example:** A fintech company uses n8n to automate loan approval workflows, reducing processing times from days to hours.

4. Apache Airflow

- **What it does:** A powerful workflow orchestration tool used to schedule, monitor, and manage complex data workflows.
- **How it works:** It helps businesses automate data pipelines, making it ideal for big data and analytics applications.
- **Example:** A media streaming service like Netflix uses Apache Airflow to manage and process terabytes of viewing data, ensuring seamless content recommendations for users.

The Role of AI in Intelligent Decision-Making

AI-powered workflow automation isn't just about executing tasks—it's also about making smarter decisions. AI can analyze vast datasets, recognize patterns, and provide recommendations, making businesses more agile and data-driven.

How AI Enables Smarter Decisions

1. **Predictive Analytics**
   - AI analyzes historical data to predict future trends, enabling businesses to make proactive decisions.
   - **Example:** A retail company uses AI to predict sales trends and adjust stock levels accordingly.
2. **Automated Data Insights**
   - AI tools can scan thousands of reports and generate summaries, saving time for decision-makers.

- Example: A CEO uses an AI-powered dashboard to get instant insights into company performance without going through lengthy reports.

3. **AI-Powered Risk Management**
    - AI detects anomalies in financial transactions, reducing the risk of fraud.
    - **Example:** A credit card company implements AI-based fraud detection, reducing fraudulent transactions by 80%.

Real-World Applications of AI-Powered Automation

The true power of AI automation is best understood through real-world applications. Let's look at some remarkable case studies:

1. Coca-Cola's AI-Powered Marketing Automation

- Coca-Cola uses AI-driven marketing automation to analyze customer preferences and create personalized campaigns.
- The system collects data from social media, purchase history, and demographics to craft highly targeted advertisements.
- **Impact:** Increased customer engagement and higher sales through tailored marketing strategies.

2. Tesla's AI-Driven Manufacturing & Logistics

- Tesla uses AI automation to manage inventory, optimize supply chain logistics, and control robotic assembly lines.
- Predictive analytics ensure that parts are ordered just in time, minimizing waste and maximizing efficiency.
- **Impact:** Faster production cycles and reduced operational costs.

3. Netflix's AI-Based Content Recommendation System

- Netflix uses AI to analyze viewing history and recommend personalized content to users.
- The system learns from user interactions and continuously refines its recommendations.
- **Impact:** Higher user retention and engagement, leading to increased revenue.

Final Thoughts: The Future of AI-Powered Workflow Automation

The future of work is AI-driven. Businesses that embrace AI-powered workflow automation will not only save time and resources but also gain a competitive edge in their industries. AI isn't replacing humans—it's empowering them to focus on more strategic and creative tasks while automation handles the repetitive work.

As AI technology continues to evolve, workflow automation will become even more intelligent, adaptive, and intuitive. Organizations that leverage these tools today will be the leaders of tomorrow. ◈

Chapter 5: The Rise of AI in Software Development

How AI is Transforming Traditional Software Development

Imagine a world where developers don't have to write thousands of lines of code manually, where software bugs are identified and fixed before they even cause problems, and where applications are built in a fraction of the time it takes today. This is not some distant future—it's already happening, thanks to AI-powered software development.

Traditional software development has always been a meticulous, time-consuming process. Developers spend countless hours writing, testing, debugging, and optimizing code. Every project follows a structured lifecycle—from planning and coding to testing and deployment. However, even the best programmers face challenges like human error, inefficiencies, and the increasing complexity of modern applications.

Enter artificial intelligence. AI is revolutionizing the way software is built, automating mundane coding tasks, enhancing code quality, and accelerating the entire development lifecycle. AI-powered tools can now assist developers by generating code snippets, offering real-time suggestions, automating software testing, and even predicting potential vulnerabilities. This transformation is not about replacing software engineers; rather, it is about empowering them to work smarter and more efficiently.

To understand the real impact of AI on software development, let's take a closer look at AI-powered coding assistants, AI-driven testing and debugging, and how these advancements are reshaping the roles of software engineers.

AI-Powered Coding Assistants

Think back to the early days of coding, when programmers had to memorize syntax and manually write every single function. Fast forward to today, and AI-powered coding assistants have become a developer's best companion. These tools help generate code, provide contextual suggestions, and even complete entire functions, making the development process significantly faster and more efficient.

Let's explore some of the top AI-powered coding assistants that are transforming software development:

1. GitHub Copilot

Imagine having an AI-powered pair programmer sitting beside you, suggesting code snippets as you type. That's exactly what GitHub Copilot does. Developed by OpenAI and GitHub, Copilot is an AI-driven coding assistant that suggests entire lines or blocks of code based on natural language prompts and previous code patterns.

- **How it works:** Copilot leverages OpenAI's Codex model, trained on billions of lines of open-source code, to provide real-time suggestions.
- **Example:** A junior developer working on a Python script for data analysis types a comment: # Function to calculate the mean of a list. Copilot instantly generates the corresponding function without the developer needing to write it manually.
- **Impact:** Copilot drastically reduces development time, helping programmers focus on solving complex problems rather than writing boilerplate code.

2. Tabnine

Tabnine takes AI-assisted coding a step further by providing personalized code suggestions tailored to a developer's coding style.

- **How it works:** It uses deep learning models trained on millions of codebases to predict and autocomplete code snippets.
- **Example:** A backend engineer working on a Node.js API sees intelligent suggestions for function implementations, reducing the effort needed to type out repetitive patterns.
- **Impact:** Tabnine improves code accuracy and consistency while accelerating development workflows.

3. Codeium

Codeium is another AI-powered coding assistant that enhances productivity by understanding natural language commands and converting them into working code.

- **How it works:** Developers can describe what they need in plain English, and Codeium generates the code accordingly.
- **Example:** A mobile developer types, "Create a function to validate email addresses," and Codeium instantly produces a properly formatted function.
- **Impact:** Codeium reduces the learning curve for new programmers while helping experienced developers write code more efficiently.

4. Amazon CodeWhisperer

Amazon's answer to AI-assisted coding, CodeWhisperer integrates seamlessly with AWS services and helps developers build cloud-native applications faster.

52

- **How it works:** It understands the context of the code being written and provides intelligent recommendations.
- **Example:** A cloud engineer working on an AWS Lambda function receives automatic suggestions for handling API requests and interacting with Amazon S3.
- **Impact:** CodeWhisperer speeds up cloud application development and ensures best practices are followed.

AI for Software Testing and Debugging

Software bugs are inevitable, but finding and fixing them has traditionally been one of the most time-consuming aspects of development. AI-powered testing and debugging tools are changing this by automating test case generation, identifying issues faster, and even predicting potential failures before they happen.

1. Diffblue

Diffblue is an AI-driven testing tool that automatically writes unit tests for Java applications, saving developers countless hours of manual testing.

- **How it works:** It analyzes existing code and generates test cases that cover all possible execution paths.
- **Example:** A fintech company using Diffblue saw a 70% reduction in time spent writing unit tests for their banking applications.
- **Impact:** Improved test coverage, fewer bugs, and faster release cycles.

2. Mabl

Mabl takes AI-driven testing to the next level by providing intelligent, self-healing automated tests.

- **How it works:** It continuously learns from test runs and adapts to changes in application UI and functionality.
- **Example:** A SaaS company deploying weekly updates uses Mabl to ensure that every new release functions correctly without manual intervention.
- **Impact:** Faster deployments and improved software reliability.

3. Testim

Testim leverages AI to streamline test automation for web and mobile applications.

- **How it works:** It learns from past test executions and optimizes test cases dynamically.
- **Example:** An e-commerce platform integrated Testim to automate checkout process testing, reducing QA efforts by 50%.
- **Impact:** Enhanced test efficiency and improved software quality.

The Impact of AI-Driven Development on Software Engineering Roles

As AI continues to reshape software development, the role of software engineers is evolving. While AI can automate coding, testing, and debugging, human expertise remains essential in multiple areas.

1. The Shift from Writing Code to Managing AI-Powered Development

- Developers are moving from manually writing every line of code to leveraging AI to generate code efficiently.

- Engineers are focusing more on architecture, security, and system design rather than low-level coding.
- **Example:** A senior software engineer now spends more time fine-tuning AI-generated code rather than writing it from scratch.

2. The Rise of AI-Enhanced Software Engineering Roles

- **AI-Assisted Developers:** Engineers who work alongside AI tools to improve productivity.
- **AI Model Trainers:** Specialists who fine-tune AI coding assistants to understand company-specific codebases.
- **AI-Driven Test Engineers:** QA professionals who leverage AI to automate testing and debugging processes.
- **Example:** A company hires an AI DevOps engineer to manage AI-generated deployment pipelines.

3. Ethical Considerations and Responsible AI Use

- AI-generated code raises concerns about bias, security vulnerabilities, and intellectual property rights.
- Developers must ensure AI-generated solutions adhere to ethical standards and secure coding practices.
- **Example:** A tech company conducts AI code reviews to identify potential security risks before deployment.

Final Thoughts: Embracing AI as a Developer's Best Friend

AI is not here to replace software engineers—it's here to empower them. The rise of AI in software development is enabling developers to work smarter, build more reliable software, and push the boundaries of innovation.

By embracing AI-powered coding assistants, automated testing tools, and AI-driven workflows, developers can focus on what truly matters—solving complex problems and building the future of technology.

The key to thriving in this AI-driven era is to adapt, learn, and integrate AI tools effectively into the development process. The future belongs to those who can leverage AI not as a competitor, but as a trusted collaborator in crafting the next generation of software solutions. ◈

Chapter 6: The Era of Autonomous Software Development

As we stand on the brink of a technological revolution, one thing is clear—AI is no longer just a tool for assisting humans in software development; it is evolving into a creator itself. The dream of fully autonomous software development, where AI not only writes but also tests, deploys, and maintains software, is turning into reality. This transformation is driven by groundbreaking innovations in AI-driven coding, AI-powered DevOps, and self-generating software agents.

In this chapter, we explore how AI is reshaping the software development landscape—from AI-assisted coding to fully autonomous software engineering. We will delve into tools like OpenAI's Codex, AutoGPT, and BabyAGI, which are pioneering the shift towards self-sustaining software development. But with great power comes great responsibility, and we will also examine the challenges, ethical considerations, and risks associated with this evolution.

From AI-Assisted Coding to Self-Generating Software

A few years ago, AI was merely a co-pilot, helping developers autocomplete lines of code or provide suggestions. But today, we are witnessing a shift where AI can autonomously generate complete software applications, significantly reducing human involvement in the development process.

Imagine a world where an AI system takes an idea and turns it into a functional application without human intervention. This is not science fiction anymore—it's happening now. Companies are already experimenting with AI models that can understand natural language descriptions of a project and generate code, user interfaces, and even deploy cloud infrastructure.

For example, a startup founder with no programming knowledge could describe their app's functionality in plain English, and an AI system could build a fully working prototype within minutes. This is the power of AI-driven autonomous software development.

The shift is happening in phases:

1. **AI-Assisted Development** – Tools like GitHub Copilot, Tabnine, and Amazon CodeWhisperer help developers by suggesting code snippets and fixing errors.
2. **AI-Generated Code** – Advanced AI models like OpenAI's Codex can generate complete functions and even entire applications based on user prompts.
3. **AI-Managed DevOps** – AI-driven automation in software deployment, testing, and maintenance is accelerating DevOps efficiency.
4. **Fully Autonomous Software Development** – AI agents like AutoGPT and BabyAGI are taking steps toward completely independent software creation, with minimal human supervision.

The Concept of AI DevOps – AI Managing Deployment, Testing, and Security

Software development doesn't end with writing code—it involves testing, deploying, monitoring, and maintaining applications. Traditionally, DevOps teams manage this process, ensuring software runs smoothly after deployment. However, AI is increasingly taking over these tasks.

How AI is Revolutionizing DevOps

1. **Automated Deployment & Monitoring**
   AI tools like **AWS DevOps Guru** and **Google Cloud**

Operations Suite analyze system logs and predict potential failures before they happen. These tools ensure high availability and minimize downtime.

2. **AI-Driven Security (DevSecOps)**
   Cybersecurity is a growing concern, and AI is now being used to detect vulnerabilities in real-time. **AI-powered security scanners** analyze codebases, identify security risks, and automatically patch vulnerabilities before they can be exploited.

3. **AI in Continuous Testing**
   Testing is one of the most time-consuming aspects of software development. AI-based tools like **Testim** and **Mabl** can generate automated test cases, execute them, and identify bugs before deployment, drastically reducing the time needed for quality assurance.

4. **Self-Healing Infrastructure**
   AI can now automatically detect and fix issues in cloud environments. If a server crashes, AI systems can instantly allocate new resources or restore previous backups without human intervention.

These advancements are paving the way for AI to take full control of software operations, making development cycles faster, more efficient, and less prone to human error.

How AI Agents Are Becoming Software Engineers

AI agents are no longer just helping developers—they are becoming developers. The emergence of **self-learning AI systems** has led to the creation of AI-powered software engineers capable of autonomously coding, debugging, and optimizing applications.

Key AI Tools Driving Autonomous Software Development

1. **OpenAI's Codex** – The brain behind GitHub Copilot, Codex can generate complex code snippets and entire applications with minimal human input. Developers can describe what they want in natural language, and Codex translates it into working code.
2. **AutoGPT** – A step beyond AI-assisted coding, AutoGPT is designed to execute tasks autonomously. It can analyze a problem, generate code, debug errors, and refine its output without human intervention.
3. **BabyAGI** – Inspired by OpenAI's AGI (Artificial General Intelligence) research, BabyAGI takes automation further by learning from past mistakes and improving its coding abilities over time. It mimics how human developers refine their skills through trial and error.

How These AI Agents Work

- **Understanding Intent:** The user provides high-level instructions or goals.
- **Breaking Down Tasks:** The AI system decomposes complex software requirements into smaller, manageable tasks.
- **Writing Code:** The AI writes and refines the code, ensuring efficiency and best practices.
- **Testing & Debugging:** The AI runs automated tests and fixes issues before deployment.
- **Deploying Software:** The AI integrates with cloud platforms to deploy the application and monitor its performance.

Real-world Example:

A fintech startup wanted to build an AI-powered chatbot for handling customer queries. Instead of hiring an entire development team, they used **AutoGPT** to generate the chatbot's code, test it, and deploy it on their website—all within 48 hours. The entire process was managed by AI with minimal human oversight.

Challenges in AI-Driven Software Development

While AI-powered software development is groundbreaking, it comes with challenges that must be addressed:

1. **Ethical & Bias Issues**
   AI models can inherit biases from their training data. If an AI agent writes biased code, it can lead to unfair outcomes in applications, particularly in industries like finance and healthcare.

2. **Security Risks**
   AI-generated software must be thoroughly vetted for vulnerabilities. Autonomous AI coding systems could introduce security flaws if not properly monitored.

3. **Dependence on Data Quality**
   AI's ability to generate high-quality code depends on the quality of its training data. Poorly trained models can produce inefficient or even erroneous code.

4. **Human Oversight is Still Needed**
   AI can write code, but it doesn't always understand business logic or the nuances of user experience. Human developers must still review and refine AI-generated applications.

5. **Legal & Compliance Challenges**
   AI-generated software may not always comply with industry regulations. Ensuring compliance in fields like healthcare, finance, and cybersecurity is a significant hurdle.

Final Thoughts: Are We Ready for Fully Autonomous Software Development?

The rise of autonomous software development is inevitable. AI agents are becoming increasingly sophisticated, capable of not just assisting but taking over entire software engineering tasks. While challenges remain, the benefits—speed, efficiency, cost reduction, and innovation—far outweigh the risks.

In the near future, we might see AI-powered companies that require little to no human developers, where software is designed, developed, and deployed by AI systems. This shift will redefine software engineering as we know it.

But one thing is certain—AI will not replace developers entirely. Instead, it will **augment human creativity**, allowing engineers to focus on high-level innovation rather than repetitive coding tasks. The future of software development is not just AI-driven; it is AI-empowered.

Chapter 7: The Business Impact of AI Agents

Artificial Intelligence (AI) agents are no longer confined to research labs or science fiction novels. They have stepped into the business world, reshaping industries, redefining customer interactions, and revolutionizing decision-making processes. AI-driven automation is not just about efficiency—it's about unlocking new levels of productivity, creating smarter enterprises, and driving economic transformation.

Imagine a world where customer service is handled instantly and efficiently by AI chatbots, where business leaders rely on AI-powered insights to make million-dollar decisions, and where entire industries are being reshaped by automation. This is no longer a vision of the future; it's happening now.

In this chapter, we will explore how AI agents are transforming businesses across sectors, revolutionizing customer support, enhancing enterprise decision-making, and even altering global economies. Through real-world case studies, we will see how companies are leveraging AI agents to achieve unprecedented success.

How AI Agents Are Reshaping Industries

Industries across the board are experiencing a paradigm shift with the adoption of AI agents. From healthcare to finance, retail to manufacturing, AI-powered automation is streamlining operations, improving customer experiences, and reducing costs. Let's take a look at some of the key industries where AI agents are making a profound impact.

1. Healthcare: AI Agents as Virtual Health Assistants

AI-powered virtual assistants are changing the way patients interact with healthcare providers. Companies like **Ada Health** and **Babylon Health** use AI to analyze symptoms and suggest possible diagnoses, reducing unnecessary doctor visits. AI-driven automation also helps hospitals manage patient records, schedule appointments, and even assist in medical imaging analysis.

◇ **Example:** During the COVID-19 pandemic, many hospitals deployed AI chatbots to handle patient inquiries, reducing the burden on frontline medical staff. **Mayo Clinic**, for instance, introduced an AI-powered chatbot to provide real-time COVID-19 updates and guidance.

2. Finance: AI in Fraud Detection & Personalized Banking

Banks and financial institutions are leveraging AI agents for fraud detection, risk assessment, and automated customer interactions. AI-driven robo-advisors, such as **Betterment** and **Wealthfront**, provide personalized investment strategies based on user preferences and market trends.

◇ **Example: JPMorgan Chase** uses an AI agent named **COIN (Contract Intelligence)** to analyze legal documents and financial contracts, saving over **360,000 hours of manual work** per year.

3. Retail & E-commerce: AI-Powered Shopping Assistants

AI agents in retail help customers find products, recommend purchases based on their preferences, and even predict shopping trends. **Amazon's Alexa** and **Walmart's AI-powered chatbots** enhance customer experience by providing voice-assisted shopping and quick order placements.

◈ **Example: Sephora** uses an AI-powered chatbot that assists customers in finding makeup products by analyzing their preferences and previous purchases.

4. Manufacturing: AI-Powered Predictive Maintenance

Manufacturing companies use AI-driven predictive maintenance to prevent machinery failures, optimize production lines, and reduce downtime. AI agents analyze sensor data and predict when equipment needs maintenance, thus preventing costly failures.

◈ **Example: Siemens** uses AI-based predictive maintenance to monitor industrial equipment, reducing maintenance costs and improving production efficiency.

5. Human Resources: AI in Hiring & Employee Engagement

Recruiters are using AI-powered tools like **HireVue** and **Pymetrics** to analyze candidates' resumes, conduct video interviews with AI-driven assessments, and match job seekers with the right roles. AI agents also assist in employee engagement by tracking performance and providing personalized career growth insights.

◈ **Example: Unilever** uses AI in recruitment to screen candidates efficiently, reducing hiring bias and improving the overall recruitment experience.

These examples highlight the transformative power of AI agents in different industries. But one of the most impactful areas where AI is driving change is in customer support.

AI-Driven Customer Support (Chatbots & Virtual Assistants)

The days of waiting on hold for customer service are fading. AI-driven chatbots and virtual assistants are handling millions of customer interactions daily, providing instant and accurate responses.

1. The Rise of AI-Powered Chatbots

AI-powered chatbots like **ChatGPT, Google Bard, and Microsoft Copilot** have evolved beyond simple question-answering. They now engage in human-like conversations, understand customer emotions, and provide contextual assistance.

◈ **Example: HDFC Bank's EVA (Electronic Virtual Assistant)** handles customer queries related to banking services, reducing wait times and improving user experience.

2. AI in Voice-Based Customer Support

Virtual assistants like **Apple's Siri, Amazon Alexa, and Google Assistant** provide hands-free, voice-enabled customer support. They help users with tasks such as setting reminders, checking account balances, and making online purchases.

◈ **Example: Domino's Pizza** uses an AI-powered voice assistant to take orders over the phone, reducing human errors and improving order efficiency.

3. AI-Powered Helpdesks for Enterprises

AI agents are also used in IT and HR helpdesks to assist employees with troubleshooting technical issues or HR-related queries.

◈ **Example: IBM's Watson Assistant** is used by businesses to automate IT support, reducing ticket resolution time and increasing employee productivity.

AI-Powered Decision-Making in Enterprises

AI agents are transforming business decision-making by analyzing massive datasets, identifying patterns, and providing actionable insights.

1. AI in Business Strategy & Market Analysis

Companies use AI-driven analytics to predict market trends, optimize pricing strategies, and identify new revenue opportunities.

◈ **Example: Netflix** uses AI algorithms to analyze viewer preferences and recommend personalized content, increasing user engagement.

2. AI in Supply Chain Optimization

AI-powered logistics systems help businesses optimize inventory, reduce waste, and improve delivery efficiency.

◈ **Example: Walmart** uses AI to predict demand fluctuations and optimize supply chain management, reducing inventory costs.

3. AI for Risk Management & Compliance

AI-powered compliance tools help businesses detect fraudulent transactions, ensure regulatory compliance, and mitigate risks.

◈ **Example: PayPal** uses AI-based fraud detection systems to analyze transaction patterns and prevent financial fraud.

Real-World Case Studies of Companies Using AI Agents

Let's look at some real-world success stories of companies leveraging AI agents for business growth.

1. Tesla's AI-Powered Manufacturing & Autonomous Vehicles

Tesla's AI-driven manufacturing processes use robots and predictive analytics to optimize production. Additionally, Tesla's self-driving AI agents continuously learn and improve through real-world data.

2. Amazon's AI-Driven Logistics & Customer Experience

Amazon's AI-powered recommendation system contributes to over **35% of its sales.** Its logistics AI ensures fast and accurate deliveries, optimizing warehouse management with robotics.

3. Google's AI in Advertising & Search

Google's AI-driven ad platform optimizes ad targeting and placement, maximizing ROI for advertisers. Its AI-powered search algorithms enhance user experience by providing highly relevant search results.

4. Uber's AI for Demand Forecasting & Driver Matching

Uber's AI predicts ride demand, adjusts pricing dynamically, and matches riders with drivers in real time, improving efficiency and profitability.

These case studies prove that AI-driven automation is not just a competitive advantage—it's a necessity for businesses to thrive in the digital era.

The Economic Impact of AI Automation

The widespread adoption of AI agents is leading to significant economic shifts:

1. **Job Transformation** – While some repetitive jobs are being automated, new opportunities are emerging in AI development, data science, and AI ethics.
2. **Cost Reduction & Productivity Boost** – AI-driven automation reduces operational costs and enhances productivity across industries.
3. **Innovation & New Business Models** – AI enables businesses to launch innovative products and services that were previously impossible.

◈ **Example:** AI automation is expected to contribute **$15.7 trillion** to the global economy by 2030 (PwC report).

Conclusion: The Future of AI Agents in Business

AI agents are no longer just an emerging technology—they are a fundamental force driving business transformation. From automating customer support to optimizing enterprise decision-making, AI is creating smarter, more efficient, and highly competitive businesses.

The key question for business leaders today is **not whether to adopt AI, but how to leverage it effectively.** Those who embrace AI-driven automation will thrive, while those who resist may struggle to keep up.

Chapter 8: The Future of No-Code/Low-Code AI in Business & Tech

For decades, software development was the exclusive domain of professional programmers. Writing lines of code, debugging errors, and building applications required years of technical expertise. But today, a seismic shift is taking place—one that is democratizing software development and placing the power of artificial intelligence (AI) in the hands of **citizen developers**.

Imagine a marketing executive building an AI-driven chatbot without writing a single line of code. A small business owner automating customer interactions with drag-and-drop AI workflows. A healthcare professional designing an AI-powered patient diagnosis tool without an engineering background. This is the promise of **no-code/low-code AI platforms**—empowering individuals across industries to harness the power of AI without deep technical knowledge.

In this chapter, we explore how no-code and low-code AI are revolutionizing business and technology, shaping the future of automation, and creating new opportunities for innovation. We'll also examine whether these platforms will replace software developers or merely redefine their roles.

The Continued Rise of No-Code/Low-Code Platforms

What Are No-Code and Low-Code AI Platforms?

Before diving into the future, let's define these terms:

- **No-code AI platforms** allow users to create AI-driven applications using a graphical interface with drag-and-drop functionality, eliminating the need for coding.

- **Low-code AI platforms** require minimal coding, enabling developers to speed up application development by integrating pre-built AI components.

These platforms are not just experimental tools; they are actively shaping industries by enabling businesses to deploy AI solutions **faster, cheaper, and more efficiently.**

Why Are No-Code/Low-Code Platforms Gaining Popularity?

Several factors are fueling the rise of no-code and low-code AI platforms:

1. **The Need for Speed:** Businesses can't afford to spend months developing AI models. No-code tools reduce development time from months to days.
2. **Shortage of Skilled Developers:** With a global shortage of AI and software engineers, businesses are turning to no-code platforms to bridge the gap.
3. **Cost-Effectiveness:** Hiring skilled AI engineers is expensive. No-code platforms significantly reduce development costs.
4. **Empowerment of Citizen Developers:** Non-technical professionals can now create AI-powered solutions, reducing dependency on IT teams.

Real-World Examples of No-Code AI in Action

- **Bubble and Adalo:** Entrepreneurs are using these no-code platforms to build AI-powered mobile and web applications.
- **ChatGPT and Jasper AI:** Marketers leverage AI writing tools to generate content without coding.
- **Zapier and Make:** Businesses automate workflows by integrating AI-powered actions across multiple applications.

As more industries embrace no-code AI, a new group of innovators is emerging—**citizen developers.**

How Citizen Developers Will Shape the Future

Who Are Citizen Developers?

A citizen developer is **a non-technical professional who creates applications using no-code/low-code tools.** They could be marketing managers, HR professionals, finance executives, or even small business owners.

Why Citizen Developers Are Game-Changers

1. **Democratizing AI:** AI is no longer restricted to engineers; anyone can build AI-powered solutions.
2. **Faster Innovation:** Citizen developers bring fresh perspectives and solve real-world problems **without waiting for IT teams.**
3. **Bridging the AI Adoption Gap:** Many businesses hesitate to adopt AI due to technical barriers. No-code platforms remove those barriers.

Case Study: How a Non-Tech Founder Built an AI-Powered Business

◈ **Example:** Sarah, a fashion entrepreneur with zero coding experience, wanted to create a **personalized AI-driven styling assistant** for her customers. Using a no-code AI platform, she built a chatbot that recommends outfits based on users' preferences. Within months, her business saw **a 40% increase in customer engagement** and **a 25% rise in sales**—all without hiring a developer.

Challenges Citizen Developers Face (And How to Overcome Them)

While no-code AI platforms are powerful, they come with challenges:

- **Limited Customization:** Pre-built templates might not always offer deep customization. Solution? Choose hybrid low-code tools when needed.
- **Security Risks:** Citizen developers must follow best practices to avoid exposing sensitive data.
- **Integration Complexities:** Connecting AI models with enterprise systems can be challenging. Solution? Use platforms with built-in integrations (e.g., Zapier).

As citizen developers reshape industries, businesses are also leveraging AI-driven **customization** to revolutionize automation.

AI-Driven Customization in Business Automation

Why Is AI Customization Critical?

Off-the-shelf AI solutions are useful, but **every business is unique**. AI-driven customization ensures that automation aligns with specific business goals, industry regulations, and customer preferences.

How No-Code AI Enables Customization

1. **Personalized Customer Experiences:** Businesses create AI-powered chatbots that provide unique responses based on user behavior.
2. **Industry-Specific Solutions:** AI agents can be tailored for **healthcare, finance, retail, and logistics**.
3. **Smart Process Automation:** Companies customize AI workflows to automate **sales, HR, marketing, and operations**.

◈ **Example: Airbnb** uses AI-powered dynamic pricing models, adjusting rental rates based on **demand, location, and customer behavior**—an example of AI-driven customization at scale.

With AI-driven automation accelerating, another major trend is emerging: **the integration of no-code AI with blockchain, IoT, and cybersecurity.**

The Integration of No-Code AI with Blockchain, IoT, and Cybersecurity

No-Code AI + Blockchain: Secure and Transparent AI

Blockchain ensures AI-generated data is **secure, immutable, and transparent.**

◈ **Example:** Companies like **Fetch.ai** and **SingularityNET** are integrating AI with blockchain to create decentralized AI marketplaces.

No-Code AI + IoT: Smarter and Connected Systems

AI-powered IoT devices **analyze real-time sensor data** without requiring developers to build custom AI models.

◈ **Example: Smart homes** use AI-powered IoT systems that **learn residents' habits** and automate lighting, heating, and security.

No-Code AI + Cybersecurity: Automating Threat Detection

Cybersecurity teams use AI-driven **no-code tools** to detect cyber threats and prevent attacks.

◈ **Example: Microsoft Defender for Endpoint** uses AI-driven security analytics to detect anomalies **without manual intervention.**

With such powerful integrations, a key question arises—will no-code AI replace software developers?

Predictions: Will No-Code AI Replace Software Developers?

The Fear vs. Reality

Many developers fear that no-code platforms will replace them. But the reality is different:

◈ **No-code AI will not replace developers. It will redefine their roles.**

How Developers Will Evolve

1. **From Coders to AI Architects:** Developers will focus on **building, optimizing, and scaling AI systems**, rather than writing repetitive code.
2. **Customization & Deep AI Models:** Businesses will still require **custom AI models, APIs, and enterprise integrations**.
3. **Security & Governance:** Developers will play a crucial role in ensuring AI compliance, security, and ethical deployment.

◈ **Example: Salesforce's Einstein AI** provides no-code AI features, but companies still hire **developers to customize workflows and integrate with enterprise systems**.

The Future: A Collaboration Between AI and Humans

Rather than fearing AI, developers should **embrace AI-powered tools** to accelerate development, reduce manual work, and **focus on creativity and problem-solving**.

Conclusion: A Future Where AI Is for Everyone

The rise of no-code/low-code AI platforms marks a **historic shift** in the way businesses build and deploy AI. From citizen developers to enterprise leaders, everyone can now leverage AI **without technical barriers.**

The future isn't about choosing between no-code AI and traditional software development. It's about creating a world where:

◈ Businesses innovate **faster**

◈ Non-technical users **harness AI's power**

◈ Developers **focus on higher-level problem-solving**

◈ **AI is no longer just for tech giants—it's for everyone.** The only question is, how will **you** use it to shape the future?

Chapter 9: How AI Agents are Reshaping Society

Imagine waking up in a world where AI-powered personal assistants handle our schedules, self-driving cars navigate bustling streets, and intelligent systems diagnose diseases faster than any doctor. This is not the distant future—it is happening now. AI agents are rapidly transforming our lives, from how we work and communicate to how we make ethical decisions.

However, as we embrace this AI revolution, we must also navigate its ethical complexities, understand its impact on employment, and ensure that AI systems are designed responsibly. This chapter explores how AI agents are reshaping society, the ethical dilemmas they bring, and how we can build a future where technology serves humanity fairly and responsibly.

The Ethical Implications of AI Automation

The Double-Edged Sword of AI

AI automation has brought immense benefits—streamlining industries, improving healthcare, and enhancing productivity. However, it also raises serious ethical concerns. The increasing reliance on AI agents poses questions about accountability, privacy, and fairness.

Who is Responsible When AI Makes a Mistake?

One of the most pressing ethical concerns is responsibility. If an AI-powered self-driving car causes an accident, who is to blame? The manufacturer? The software developer? The car owner? The lack of clear accountability makes it difficult to determine responsibility, highlighting the need for robust AI governance.

◈ **Example:** In 2018, an autonomous Uber vehicle struck and killed a pedestrian in Arizona. The incident sparked global debates about AI accountability and safety.

The Privacy Dilemma: How Much Data is Too Much?

AI agents thrive on data. The more they learn about us, the better they can serve us. However, this also means that they collect vast amounts of personal data, raising concerns about privacy and security.

◈ **Example:** AI-powered virtual assistants like Amazon Alexa and Google Assistant continuously listen for commands, but concerns about them recording private conversations have led to heated discussions about surveillance and data misuse.

Addressing Ethical Challenges

To ensure ethical AI automation, businesses and governments must:

1. **Implement AI ethics frameworks** that define responsibilities and transparency in decision-making.
2. **Enforce data protection regulations** to prevent misuse of personal information.
3. **Develop AI systems that prioritize human well-being** rather than just efficiency and profit.

The Impact of AI Agents on Jobs and Employment

Will AI Take Our Jobs?

One of the most debated topics in AI is its effect on employment. While AI automates repetitive tasks, it also creates new job opportunities that never existed before. The challenge is not job loss, but job transition.

Jobs Most Affected by AI Automation

Some industries are more vulnerable to AI automation than others:

- **Manufacturing:** Robotics and AI-driven automation have replaced many assembly-line jobs.
- **Customer Service:** AI chatbots now handle a significant share of customer interactions.
- **Transportation:** Self-driving technology threatens the jobs of millions of drivers worldwide.

◈ **Example:** Amazon's warehouses use AI-powered robots to sort and pack items, reducing reliance on human workers while increasing efficiency.

New Job Opportunities Created by AI

While AI eliminates some jobs, it also creates new ones:

- **AI Trainers:** People who train AI models to improve accuracy.
- **Ethical AI Officers:** Professionals ensuring AI systems adhere to ethical guidelines.
- **AI System Auditors:** Experts who monitor AI decision-making for fairness and bias.

How to Adapt to the AI Job Market

The key to thriving in an AI-driven job market is continuous learning. Professionals should:

1. **Develop AI literacy** to understand and work alongside AI systems.
2. **Focus on uniquely human skills** like creativity, emotional intelligence, and problem-solving.
3. **Seek careers that integrate AI** rather than compete with it.

AI Governance and Regulations: The Need for Responsible AI

Why AI Needs Regulation

AI is evolving faster than regulations can keep up. Without clear rules, unethical AI practices can lead to discrimination, privacy breaches, and even safety hazards.

◈ **Example:** In 2019, the Netherlands government faced criticism when an AI system falsely accused thousands of people of fraud in welfare claims, demonstrating the dangers of unregulated AI.

Key Areas of AI Governance

1. **Transparency:** AI systems should explain their decisions in understandable terms.
2. **Accountability:** Clear responsibility must be assigned when AI makes mistakes.
3. **Bias Prevention:** AI must be trained on diverse datasets to ensure fairness.
4. **Data Protection:** Regulations like GDPR must be enforced to safeguard user data.

Global Efforts in AI Regulation

Governments worldwide are beginning to implement AI regulations:

- The **EU AI Act** aims to establish strict rules for high-risk AI applications.
- The **U.S. AI Bill of Rights** proposes guidelines for ethical AI use.
- China has introduced **AI transparency laws** to monitor AI decision-making.

However, global collaboration is essential to prevent regulatory loopholes and ensure AI serves humanity ethically.

AI Bias and Fairness: How to Build Ethical AI Systems

The Problem of AI Bias

AI systems are only as good as the data they are trained on. If biased data is used, AI models can perpetuate and even amplify discrimination.

◈ **Example:** A hiring AI tool used by Amazon was found to discriminate against female applicants because it was trained on resumes that favored men.

How to Ensure AI Fairness

1. **Diverse and Representative Training Data:** AI must be trained on data that reflects different demographics.
2. **Regular Bias Audits:** AI systems should be tested for biases before deployment.
3. **Inclusive AI Development Teams:** AI teams should consist of diverse members to prevent unintentional biases.
4. **Ethical AI Policies:** Organizations must establish strict guidelines on AI fairness and inclusivity.

The Role of Humans in AI Fairness

While AI can process vast amounts of data, human oversight is crucial to ensure ethical decision-making. AI should **augment** human judgment, not replace it.

The Social Transformation Driven by AI-Powered Automation

How AI is Changing Everyday Life

AI is not just transforming industries—it is reshaping society at a fundamental level.

1. **Education:** AI-driven learning platforms personalize education based on students' strengths and weaknesses.
2. **Healthcare:** AI-powered diagnostics and robotic surgeries are improving patient outcomes.
3. **Social Good:** AI is being used to predict natural disasters, combat climate change, and provide accessibility solutions for people with disabilities.

◈ **Example:** Google's AI-powered flood forecasting system has helped communities prepare for floods, saving countless lives.

The Future of an AI-Powered Society

AI has the potential to:

- Reduce human error in critical fields like healthcare and security.
- Free humans from mundane tasks, allowing them to focus on creativity and innovation.
- Improve accessibility and inclusivity, making technology available to everyone.

However, to achieve this future, **ethical AI development, responsible governance, and continuous human oversight** are essential.

Conclusion: Shaping a Future Where AI and Humans Coexist

AI is not inherently good or bad—it is a tool that reflects the intentions of those who create and deploy it. As AI agents reshape society, we must ensure they do so **ethically, responsibly, and inclusively**.

The future is not about choosing between humans and AI but about designing AI that enhances human potential while safeguarding our values. The question is not whether AI will change our world—it already has. The real question is: **How will we guide AI to create a better future for all?**

Chapter 10: The Next Frontier – AI Agents in the Metaverse & Web3

The Digital Renaissance: AI Agents Meet the Metaverse & Web3

Imagine waking up in the morning, putting on your lightweight AR glasses, and stepping into a virtual workspace where your AI agent has already prepared a personalized briefing. It has analyzed market trends, scheduled your meetings, and even negotiated deals with other AI-powered entities across the decentralized web. This isn't science fiction—it's the emerging reality of AI in the Metaverse and Web3.

As we stand at the cusp of this new era, the convergence of AI, Blockchain, and the Metaverse is shaping a digital universe where intelligent agents will not just assist but autonomously operate within virtual worlds, business ecosystems, and decentralized applications.

The Convergence of AI, Blockchain, and the Metaverse

Over the past decade, three technological waves have been evolving in parallel—AI, Blockchain, and the Metaverse. Each of these alone has been revolutionary, but together, they hold the power to redefine digital interaction, ownership, and automation.

- **AI**: The intelligence layer that enables decision-making, automation, and learning in digital environments.
- **Blockchain**: The trust layer that ensures transparency, security, and decentralization.
- **Metaverse**: The experience layer where digital interactions take place, blurring the line between physical and virtual reality.

This convergence means that AI agents will soon be operating as autonomous entities in digital spaces, executing transactions, creating content, and interacting with users in ways we've never seen before.

How AI Agents Will Power Virtual Worlds & Web3 Applications

1. AI-Powered Virtual Assistants in the Metaverse

Virtual assistants today, like Alexa or Siri, are reactive—they wait for input and execute predefined actions. However, in the Metaverse, AI-powered agents will proactively assist users in a fully immersive way.

◈ *Imagine an AI concierge in the Metaverse, tailored to your personality. It helps you navigate digital spaces, recommends investments in virtual real estate, and even assists in managing your digital identity across multiple platforms.*

Companies like **Meta, NVIDIA Omniverse, and Decentraland** are already integrating AI into virtual environments, where AI avatars can interact, trade digital assets, and learn user behaviors to enhance experiences.

2. Decentralized AI – The Role of Blockchain in AI Agent Development

One of the biggest challenges in AI today is **data centralization**—tech giants control vast amounts of user data, raising privacy concerns. Blockchain-based AI changes the game by enabling decentralized AI models that operate securely without a central authority.

◈ *Example: Fetch.AI is a blockchain-powered AI network that allows autonomous agents to interact and transact in a decentralized manner.*

Decentralized AI will ensure that AI models remain open-source, secure, and transparent. Instead of relying on a single corporation, AI systems will operate on community-driven networks, where users collectively own and govern the data.

3. AI-Driven Smart Contracts & Autonomous Digital Transactions

Blockchain introduced the concept of smart contracts—self-executing contracts that run on decentralized networks. Now, with the infusion of AI, these contracts will evolve into intelligent, self-improving agreements that adapt to new conditions.

◈ *For instance, an AI-driven smart contract could analyze supply chain conditions and autonomously negotiate pricing based on real-time market trends, ensuring optimized and fair trade deals without human intervention.*

Platforms like **SingularityNET** and **Ocean Protocol** are pioneering this fusion, enabling AI-powered decision-making within decentralized applications (dApps).

4. The Rise of AI-Powered Virtual Influencers & Digital Humans

AI-generated influencers like **Lil Miquela and Imma** have already disrupted the influencer marketing space, but what if these virtual beings could autonomously evolve, interact, and develop their own personalities?

In the Metaverse, AI agents will not only exist as static virtual assistants but as **fully independent digital entities** that learn, adapt, and engage with real users dynamically.

◈ *Imagine an AI-powered musician in the Metaverse, composing songs based on audience emotions in real time, performing in virtual concerts, and even collaborating with human artists across different digital worlds.*

Companies like **Synthesia, Replika, and Soul Machines** are creating digital humans with lifelike emotions, enabling a new form of interaction in both entertainment and business settings.

Challenges & Ethical Considerations

While the future of AI in the Metaverse and Web3 is promising, it comes with its set of challenges:

- **Data Ownership & Privacy**: Who owns the data AI agents collect in decentralized environments?
- **AI Bias & Ethics**: Ensuring that AI agents do not inherit biases or exploit users in virtual worlds.
- **Security & Fraud Prevention**: With AI-driven financial transactions, how do we prevent malicious AI activity?

The road ahead will require **strong governance models**, ethical AI frameworks, and robust regulations to ensure that AI-powered digital worlds remain fair, inclusive, and safe for all users.

The Future of AI Agents in the Metaverse

As we move forward, AI agents will continue to evolve, transforming how we interact with digital environments. Some exciting possibilities include:

◈ **AI-powered decentralized economies** where AI agents create and trade digital assets autonomously.

◈ **Personalized Metaverse experiences** where AI learns from user preferences to design unique virtual worlds.

◈ **Self-learning AI systems** that evolve through real-time interactions, adapting to new challenges dynamically.

The next decade will be **an era of intelligent, self-operating digital ecosystems**, where AI agents play a central role in shaping how we live, work, and interact in virtual spaces.

Conclusion: The Dawn of a New Digital Era

The fusion of **AI, Blockchain, and the Metaverse** is ushering in a digital revolution where AI agents will no longer just assist but independently operate within decentralized environments. Whether in finance, entertainment, healthcare, or business, **AI-powered agents will be the architects of the next digital economy.**

This transformation is **not just about technology—it's about how we redefine digital ownership, automation, and human-AI collaboration in an increasingly interconnected world.**

◈ *Are we ready for a future where AI agents autonomously build, trade, and interact in digital worlds? The answer lies in how we embrace and shape this evolution today.*

Chapter 11: The Road to Fully Autonomous AI Systems

The Dawn of a New Era: AI's Journey to Full Autonomy

Imagine waking up in a world where AI-driven systems autonomously manage cities, optimize global resources, and even make complex governance decisions. A world where artificial intelligence doesn't just assist humans—it thinks, learns, and acts independently, solving challenges at a scale beyond human capability. While this may sound like a futuristic dream, we are already on the path to creating fully autonomous AI systems that will reshape every aspect of our world.

The road to fully autonomous AI is both exhilarating and daunting. As we edge closer to Artificial General Intelligence (AGI), we must navigate the opportunities and risks with wisdom and responsibility. This chapter explores how AI is progressing toward full autonomy, the impact it will have on decision-making, the potential dangers, and how individuals and businesses can prepare for this AI-driven future.

The Vision of General AI (AGI) and Autonomous AI Agents

The concept of AI has evolved significantly over the decades. Today, we mostly work with **Narrow AI**—systems designed to perform specific tasks, such as voice assistants, recommendation engines, and self-driving cars. However, the ultimate goal is to develop **Artificial General Intelligence (AGI)**—AI that can think, learn, and adapt across multiple domains, just like a human.

How Close Are We to AGI?

While AGI is still in its early theoretical stages, rapid advancements in deep learning, reinforcement learning, and neural networks indicate that it could become a reality within the next few decades. Companies like OpenAI, DeepMind, and Anthropic are pushing the boundaries of AI research, developing models that can:

◈ Understand and generate human-like text with remarkable accuracy (e.g., GPT models). ◈ Play complex strategy games better than human grandmasters (e.g., AlphaGo, AlphaZero). ◈ Create and optimize code autonomously (e.g., GitHub Copilot).

The Role of Autonomous AI Agents

Autonomous AI agents are already making strides in various fields. For example:

- **AI in Finance:** Algorithmic trading bots autonomously analyze market trends and execute trades at lightning speed.
- **AI in Healthcare:** AI-driven diagnostics can detect diseases in medical scans with higher accuracy than human doctors.
- **AI in Logistics:** Self-optimizing supply chain networks reduce costs and improve efficiency without human intervention.

These are only the first steps. Future AI agents will not just assist humans but will operate with full autonomy, making decisions that impact industries and societies at large.

How AI Will Surpass Human Decision-Making in Key Areas

The ability of AI to process vast amounts of data, recognize patterns, and make objective decisions gives it an edge over human cognition. Here's how AI is poised to outperform human decision-making in critical domains:

1. Healthcare: Predictive Diagnosis & Precision Medicine

AI-powered medical systems can analyze millions of patient records, genetic profiles, and real-time health data to predict diseases before they manifest.

◈ *Example: IBM Watson once analyzed thousands of leukemia cases and recommended treatment plans that human doctors had overlooked.*

2. Climate Change & Environmental Protection

AI can model climate scenarios, optimize renewable energy distribution, and even combat deforestation through automated monitoring.

◈ *Example: AI-driven satellite imagery analysis by companies like Planet Labs is helping track illegal logging in real time.*

3. Governance & Policy Making

Governments worldwide are exploring AI-driven policy recommendations that eliminate human biases and optimize resource allocation.

◈ *Example: Estonia's e-government system uses AI to automate bureaucratic processes, making governance more efficient.*

4. Autonomous Vehicles & Smart Cities

Self-driving cars, AI-managed traffic control systems, and smart city infrastructure will reduce congestion and accidents while optimizing urban planning.

◈ *Example: Tesla's Full Self-Driving (FSD) technology aims to make roads safer by eliminating human error from driving.*

These advancements suggest that AI will not just support decision-making—it will make decisions **faster, more accurately, and more objectively** than humans ever could.

The Risks and Challenges of Full AI Autonomy

While the vision of autonomous AI is exciting, it also presents significant challenges:

1. Loss of Human Control

If AI systems become fully autonomous, how do we ensure they align with human values? The risk of **misaligned AI** could lead to unintended consequences.

◈ *Example: The infamous "paperclip maximizer" thought experiment suggests an AI optimized for making paperclips might consume all resources to achieve its goal.*

2. Job Displacement & Economic Inequality

Autonomous AI will undoubtedly replace certain jobs, raising concerns about mass unemployment and economic disruption.

◈ *Example: AI-powered automation in manufacturing and customer service has already reduced the need for human workers in many industries.*

3. Bias & Ethical Concerns

AI models trained on biased data can perpetuate discrimination and social inequalities.

⚖ *Example: Studies have shown that facial recognition AI exhibits racial biases, leading to wrongful arrests and unfair treatment.*

4. Cybersecurity Threats

Autonomous AI systems, if hacked, could cause catastrophic failures in financial systems, national security, and critical infrastructure.

◇ *Example: AI-powered cyberattacks could manipulate financial markets or disrupt power grids.*

AI's Role in Solving Global Challenges

Despite these risks, AI holds immense potential to tackle the world's most pressing problems. Here's how:

◇ Fighting Climate Change

- AI can optimize renewable energy production, improve energy efficiency, and reduce carbon emissions.
- Google's DeepMind has helped cut power usage in data centers by 40% through AI-driven energy management.

◇ Advancing Healthcare

- AI-driven drug discovery is accelerating vaccine development and finding cures for diseases.
- DeepMind's AlphaFold solved the protein-folding problem, unlocking breakthroughs in medicine.

◇ Enhancing Governance & Social Equity

- AI-powered analytics can reduce corruption and ensure fair policy-making by analyzing massive datasets objectively.
- Predictive policing (if implemented ethically) can help law enforcement prevent crimes before they occur.

AI, when developed responsibly, has the power to reshape the world for the better.

Preparing for an AI-Driven Future: What Businesses and Individuals Should Do

◈ **For Businesses:**

◈ Invest in AI upskilling programs for employees.

◈ Implement AI ethically with clear governance policies. ◈ Leverage AI for efficiency while maintaining human oversight.

◈◈ **For Individuals:**

◈ Adapt by learning AI-related skills (coding, data science, ethics in AI).

◈ Stay informed about AI developments and regulations. ◈ Focus on uniquely human skills like creativity, emotional intelligence, and strategic thinking.

The transition to an AI-driven world will require businesses and individuals to evolve continuously.

Conclusion: Embracing the AI-Driven Future Responsibly

The road to fully autonomous AI systems is both **exciting and uncertain.** AI has the potential to **outperform human decision-making, solve global challenges**, and **drive economic growth**, but it also poses risks that must be managed carefully. As we move closer to AGI, we must ensure that AI remains a force for good, governed by ethical principles and human oversight.

The future isn't about AI versus humans—it's about **AI augmenting human potential.** The question isn't whether AI will take over, but how we can **coexist and collaborate with AI to build a better future for all.**

◇ *Are we ready to embrace this revolution? The time to prepare is now.*

Chapter 12: Embracing the AI Agent Revolution – The Path Forward

The world is standing at the threshold of an AI-driven era. The revolution isn't coming—it's already here, transforming the way businesses operate, how individuals work, and how societies function. But where do we go from here? How do we prepare for this paradigm shift where human intelligence and AI agents work together to create something even greater?

In this final chapter, we will explore the path forward—how individuals, businesses, and societies can embrace AI, not just as a tool, but as an integral part of the future.

The New Paradigm of Human-AI Collaboration

For centuries, technological advancements have reshaped industries, and every major breakthrough—from the steam engine to the internet—has raised concerns about job displacement. AI is no different. However, unlike previous innovations, AI is not just automating manual tasks; it's evolving into an intellectual partner, augmenting human decision-making and creativity.

Imagine a lawyer preparing for a major case. Traditionally, they would sift through thousands of pages of legal documents, searching for precedents and relevant cases. Today, AI-driven legal assistants like Harvey or Casetext can analyze legal texts in seconds, highlighting critical information and providing strategic recommendations. The lawyer is still in control, but their efficiency has multiplied exponentially.

Similarly, in marketing, AI is not replacing creative directors but enhancing their capabilities. AI-driven tools analyze market trends, personalize advertising campaigns, and predict consumer behavior, allowing professionals to focus on strategy and storytelling.

The collaboration between AI and humans is not about competition but augmentation. The professionals who learn to work *with* AI will outpace those who resist it.

How to Adapt to AI Collaboration

1. **Recognize AI as a Partner, Not a Threat** – Instead of fearing AI, professionals must understand how it enhances their roles.
2. **Experiment with AI Tools** – Hands-on experience with AI-powered applications in your industry will demystify its use and build confidence.
3. **Develop Hybrid Skills** – Combining domain expertise with AI literacy will make professionals indispensable in the workforce.

How Businesses Can Prepare for AI-First Operations

Businesses that embrace AI agents today will be the leaders of tomorrow. AI is no longer an experimental technology reserved for tech giants—it is becoming a core component of operations across industries.

Take the example of Amazon. Their AI-driven supply chain management ensures that millions of products are delivered efficiently worldwide. AI optimizes warehouse storage, predicts demand patterns, and automates logistics, making operations seamless.

Similarly, financial institutions are leveraging AI for fraud detection, risk management, and customer service automation. JPMorgan Chase, for instance, uses AI to analyze contract documents in seconds—work that would take legal teams thousands of hours.

So, how can businesses integrate AI into their workflows?

Steps for Businesses to Become AI-First

1. **Assess AI Readiness** – Evaluate which processes in your organization can be automated or enhanced with AI.
2. **Invest in AI Training** – Upskilling employees to work with AI ensures smoother adoption and maximized benefits.
3. **Start Small, Scale Fast** – Begin with small AI-driven projects and scale them as confidence and efficiency improve.
4. **Integrate AI into Decision-Making** – AI should not be limited to automation; it should actively contribute to business strategy and innovation.

The Importance of AI Education and Reskilling

AI is reshaping job roles, making AI literacy as critical as digital literacy once was. Individuals who adapt will thrive, while those who resist may struggle to keep up.

Think about it—just a decade ago, social media marketing was not a mainstream profession. Today, it is a core function in every organization. AI-related roles will follow the same trajectory. From AI ethics consultants to AI trainers, new job titles will emerge, creating opportunities for those who are prepared.

How Individuals Can Prepare for an AI-Driven Workforce

1. **Learn AI Basics** – Even if you are not a developer, understanding how AI works will help you stay relevant in your profession.
2. **Reskill and Upskill** – Courses on AI, data science, and automation are widely available. Online platforms like Coursera, Udacity, and LinkedIn Learning offer AI literacy

programs.

3. **Stay Curious and Open-Minded** – AI is evolving rapidly. Being adaptable and continuously learning will keep you ahead of the curve.

4. **Develop a Problem-Solving Mindset** – AI tools are only as effective as the people guiding them. The ability to frame problems and ask the right questions will be invaluable.

Final Thoughts on AI's Role in Shaping the Future

AI is not just about automation—it's about *amplification*. It is enhancing human intelligence, accelerating innovation, and transforming the way we work, live, and think.

Consider how AI is helping in critical areas like healthcare. AI-driven diagnostics are detecting diseases earlier and with greater accuracy. IBM Watson Health, for example, has revolutionized cancer treatment planning by analyzing medical literature and patient data to recommend personalized treatments.

In education, AI is making learning more accessible. Platforms like Duolingo use AI to personalize language learning, adapting lessons to each user's pace and style.

Even in creative fields, AI is collaborating with artists and musicians. AI-generated art and music are not replacing human creativity but expanding its possibilities.

The future of AI is not a dystopian world where machines take over. It is a world where humans and AI collaborate to push the boundaries of what's possible.

Call to Action: How Readers Can Leverage AI Agents for Success

As we conclude this book, the most important question is: *What will you do with AI?*

The AI Agent Revolution is not a trend—it is the new reality. The time to embrace AI is now. Whether you are a business leader, a student, a professional, or an entrepreneur, AI can be your most powerful ally.

Steps to Take Today

1. **Explore AI Tools** – Experiment with AI-powered platforms relevant to your industry.
2. **Join AI Communities** – Engage with AI professionals, attend AI meetups, and participate in discussions to stay updated.
3. **Start an AI Project** – Apply AI to a small project in your field. The best way to learn is by doing.
4. **Advocate for Responsible AI** – Promote ethical AI development and use, ensuring that AI is inclusive and beneficial for all.

The future belongs to those who adapt, innovate, and lead. AI is not here to replace you—it is here to empower you.

Are you ready to embrace the AI Agent Revolution?

Let's shape the future, together.

Conclusion

As I sit back and reflect on the journey we have taken through this book, one thing becomes crystal clear—the AI revolution is not just about technology. It's about *people*. It's about *you*, me, and how we choose to shape the future with the tools at our disposal.

We've explored the profound transformation AI agents are bringing to industries, businesses, and our everyday lives. From revolutionizing healthcare and finance to redefining education and creativity, AI is no longer a distant dream—it's here, *now*, changing the very fabric of our world.

But with this transformation comes responsibility. AI is a double-edged sword—one that holds the promise of boundless innovation yet demands careful stewardship. How we navigate this new landscape will determine whether AI remains a force for good or becomes a challenge that spirals beyond our control.

Let's take a moment to reflect on the key lessons we've uncovered throughout this book.

1. AI is Here to Empower, Not Replace

If there's one thing I want you to take away, it's this—AI is not the enemy. It is not here to steal jobs or diminish human potential. Instead, AI is an *amplifier* of human capability.

Think about how AI-powered assistants are enabling doctors to diagnose diseases faster, how AI-driven analytics are helping businesses make smarter decisions, and how generative AI is allowing artists and writers to push the boundaries of creativity.

The professionals, businesses, and leaders who embrace AI as a *collaborator* rather than a competitor will thrive. The future belongs to those who see AI as an *opportunity*, not a threat.

So ask yourself—how can you *leverage* AI to unlock new possibilities in your work and life?

2. The Future of Work is Human + AI Collaboration

The traditional workforce is evolving at an unprecedented pace. AI agents are taking over repetitive, time-consuming tasks, allowing humans to focus on what truly matters—*critical thinking, creativity, and strategy*.

But this transition is not automatic. It requires *adaptation*. The people who continuously learn, reskill, and embrace AI tools will find themselves ahead of the curve, while those who resist may struggle to keep up.

The question is not whether AI will be a part of your job—it will. The real question is: *How prepared are you to work alongside AI?*

Now is the time to invest in *AI literacy, reskilling*, and *lifelong learning*. The more we understand AI, the better equipped we are to harness its power for good.

3. AI Must Be Built Ethically and Responsibly

With great power comes great responsibility. AI is shaping decisions that affect lives—whether it's a loan approval, a medical diagnosis, or a hiring process. If AI systems are built with bias, lack transparency, or fall into the wrong hands, they can do more harm than good.

That's why ethical AI development is not just a technical challenge—it's a *human* one. Governments, businesses, and individuals must come together to ensure AI is used fairly, equitably, and transparently.

Each of us has a role to play. As a business leader, you can ensure your AI systems are inclusive. As a policymaker, you can advocate for responsible AI governance. As a consumer, you can demand ethical AI practices from the companies you support.

The future of AI is in *our* hands. What kind of AI-driven world do we want to create?

4. AI is Reshaping Society—Are You Ready for the Change?

AI is not just transforming industries—it is *reshaping society itself*. From AI-powered education and hyper-personalized healthcare to AI-driven governance and automation, the way we live, interact, and make decisions is undergoing a radical shift.

Some changes will be disruptive. Some will be challenging. But *every great transformation in history has come with uncertainty*. The key is to stay *agile*, *informed*, and *proactive*.

The individuals and organizations that embrace AI-driven transformation with *curiosity* rather than *fear* will be the pioneers of the new era. Will you be one of them?

5. This is Just the Beginning—The Best is Yet to Come

We are still in the early days of the AI revolution. The breakthroughs we have seen so far—from ChatGPT to AI-powered robotics—are just the *foundation* of what's to come. The next decade will bring advances that today seem like science fiction.

Imagine a world where AI agents manage entire cities, optimize global supply chains, and drive scientific discoveries at an unprecedented pace. Imagine AI helping us solve humanity's biggest challenges—curing diseases, tackling climate change, and ensuring sustainable growth for future generations.

That world is not far away. But it is up to *us* to decide how we shape it.

Your Next Step: Become a Leader in the AI Era

This book was never just about understanding AI—it was about *empowering you* to take action.

So now, I ask you—*what will you do with the knowledge you have gained?*

Will you explore AI tools and start integrating them into your work?

Will you invest in learning about AI and staying ahead of the curve?

Will you become an advocate for responsible AI and ethical innovation?

The future does not belong to those who wait. It belongs to those who *act*.

The AI Agent Revolution is here. Are you ready to lead the way?

Final Words

As I conclude this journey, I want to leave you with a thought—**AI is not just about technology. It's about human potential.**

We stand at a crossroads where AI can be the greatest force for innovation, creativity, and progress that humanity has ever seen. But its true impact will not be determined by the algorithms or machines—it will be determined by *us*.

Let's not fear the future. Let's *shape* it.

Let's embrace the AI revolution *together* and create a world where technology amplifies our abilities, expands our possibilities, and uplifts humanity to new heights.

The future is calling. Let's answer it—boldly, intelligently, and ethically.

Let's build the AI-powered world we truly deserve.

References

1. **Meta's Brave New Horizons**
   https://www.ft.com/content/df26fc4c-5488-4994-b2b8-be4bfbda2724

2. **AI Agents Are Everywhere...and Nowhere**
   https://www.wsj.com/articles/ai-agents-are-everywhereand-nowhere-87e38703

3. **China's BYD Goes All-In on Self-Driving, with Even Its $9,500 EV Getting 'High-Level' Autonomous Features**
   https://www.businessinsider.com/byd-self-driving-expansion-cheap-seagull-ev-high-level-features-2025-2

4. **AI Wants to Google for You**
   https://www.vox.com/technology/399512/ai-open-ai-operator-agents-paris-aiaction-summit

5. **Internal Memo: Meta is Betting on Humanoid Robots and Hires the Former CEOs of Cruise and The RealReal**
   https://www.businessinsider.com/leaked-memo-meta-humanoid-robots-hires-ex-cruise-realreal-ceo-2025-2

6. **AI Agents in Web3: From Hype to Revolution**
   https://subquery.medium.com/ai-agents-in-web3-from-hype-to-revolution-15645757338a

7. **What Is Autonomous AI?**
   https://www.techtarget.com/searchenterpriseai/definition/autonomous-artificial-intelligence-autonomous-AI

8. **Decoding the Role of Artificial Intelligence in Metaverse and Web3**
   https://www.quillaudits.com/blog/ai-agents/ai-in-metaverse-web3

9. **Autonomous Artificial Intelligence Guide: The Future of AI**

https://www.algotive.ai/blog/autonomous-artificial-intelligence-guide-the-future-of-ai

10. **AI Agents Could Be the Next Tech Hype Bubble to Burst, Say VCs**
https://sifted.eu/articles/ai-agents-bubble

11. **Truly Autonomous AI is on the Horizon**
https://www.eurekalert.org/news-releases/1073232

12. **What Possibilities is the AI Agent Bringing to the Metaverse and Web3**
https://www.chaincatcher.com/en/article/2161799

13. **From Manual to Fully Autonomous: The 5 Levels of AI Testing**
https://medium.com/%40gururajhm/from-manual-to-fully-autonomous-the-5-levels-of-ai-testing-ae3080122e85

14. **AI Agents Transforming the Web3 User Experience**
https://www.biconomy.io/post/ai-agents-transforming-the-web3-user-experience

15. **How Does AI Drive Autonomous Systems?**
https://scienceexchange.caltech.edu/topics/artificial-intelligence-research/autonomous-ai-cars-drones

16. **Can AI Agents Bloom in VR?**
https://medium.com/exponential-era/can-ai-agents-bloom-in-the-metaverse-639d842854f6

17. **Autonomous AI Agents Are Coming: Why Trust and Training Hold the Keys to Their Success**
https://www.salesforce.com/news/stories/ai-training-trust/

18. **What Possibilities Does AI Agent Bring to the Metaverse and Web3**
https://followin.io/en/feed/15562873

19. **The Autonomous Systems Pattern of AI**
https://www.forbes.com/sites/cognitiveworld/2020/05/30/the-autonomous-systems-pattern-of-ai/

20. A Complete Guide to AI Agents: The Next Web3 Revolution
    https://nftplazas.com/ai-agents-guide/
21. Fully Autonomous AI Agents Are a Reckless Experiment
    https://medium.com/physics-and-machine-learning/fully-autonomous-ai-agents-are-a-reckless-experiment-e1e4f274c760
22. What is Autonomous AI?
    https://www.polymersearch.com/glossary/autonomous-ai
23. SuperDriverAI: Towards Design and Implementation for End-to-End Learning-based Autonomous Driving
    https://arxiv.org/abs/2305.10443

Glossary of Terms

A

- **AI Agent** – A software program or system powered by artificial intelligence that can autonomously perform tasks, make decisions, and interact with humans or other systems.
- **Artificial General Intelligence (AGI)** – A hypothetical AI system with human-like cognitive abilities, capable of understanding, learning, and applying knowledge across a wide range of tasks without human intervention.
- **Artificial Intelligence (AI)** – The simulation of human intelligence in machines, enabling them to perform tasks such as problem-solving, pattern recognition, decision-making, and natural language processing.
- **Automation** – The use of technology, including AI, to perform tasks without human intervention, often increasing efficiency and accuracy.

B

- **Big Data** – Extremely large datasets that require advanced tools and techniques, such as AI and machine learning, for processing, analysis, and extracting meaningful insights.
- **Bot** – A software application that runs automated tasks over the internet, including AI-powered chatbots that assist users in customer service and information retrieval.

C

- **Chatbot** – An AI-powered software application that interacts with users through text or voice, often used in customer support, sales, and virtual assistance.

- **Cloud Computing** – The delivery of computing services, including storage, processing, and AI capabilities, over the internet, allowing businesses to scale their operations without physical infrastructure.
- **Computer Vision** – A field of AI that enables machines to interpret and process visual data, such as images and videos, similar to human vision.

D

- **Deep Learning** – A subset of machine learning that uses neural networks with multiple layers to process complex patterns in data, enabling AI systems to perform tasks like image recognition and language translation.
- **Digital Transformation** – The process of integrating digital technologies, including AI, into all aspects of business and society to improve efficiency, innovation, and customer experiences.
- **Data Science** – The discipline of extracting insights and knowledge from structured and unstructured data using statistical, computational, and AI techniques.

E

- **Edge AI** – AI systems that process data locally on devices (such as smartphones, IoT devices, or self-driving cars) rather than relying on cloud-based computations, reducing latency and improving performance.
- **Ethical AI** – The practice of developing AI systems that are transparent, fair, unbiased, and aligned with ethical principles

to prevent harm and ensure responsible use.

F

- **Federated Learning** – A machine learning technique where AI models are trained across multiple decentralized devices or servers while keeping data localized to ensure privacy.
- **Fine-Tuning** – The process of improving an AI model's performance by training it on specific datasets to enhance accuracy and relevance for a particular application.

G

- **Generative AI** – AI models capable of generating new content, such as text, images, and code, based on training data. Examples include ChatGPT, DALL·E, and Midjourney.
- **GPT (Generative Pre-trained Transformer)** – A type of AI language model that generates human-like text based on a given input, widely used for chatbots, content generation, and automation.

H

- **Hyperautomation** – The use of AI, machine learning, and robotic process automation (RPA) to automate business processes end-to-end, reducing manual intervention.
- **Human-in-the-Loop (HITL)** – A model where human oversight is included in AI decision-making processes to ensure accuracy, ethics, and quality control.

I

- **Intelligent Automation (IA)** – The combination of AI,

machine learning, and automation technologies to enable systems to make decisions and execute tasks with minimal human intervention.

- **Internet of Things (IoT)** – A network of interconnected devices that collect and exchange data over the internet, often enhanced by AI for real-time analysis and automation.

L

- **Large Language Model (LLM)** – An advanced AI model trained on vast amounts of text data to understand and generate human-like language. Examples include OpenAI's GPT, Google Gemini, and Meta's Llama.
- **Low-Code/No-Code AI** – AI development platforms that allow users to build applications and automate processes without extensive programming knowledge.

M

- **Machine Learning (ML)** – A subset of AI that enables machines to learn from data and improve their performance over time without explicit programming.
- **Model Training** – The process of feeding data into an AI system to improve its ability to recognize patterns, make predictions, or automate tasks.

N

- **Natural Language Processing (NLP)** – A branch of AI that enables computers to understand, interpret, and respond to human language, commonly used in chatbots, sentiment analysis, and translation tools.

- **Neural Networks** – AI models inspired by the human brain, consisting of interconnected nodes that process data to recognize patterns and make decisions.

O

- **Optical Character Recognition (OCR)** – AI-powered technology that converts printed or handwritten text into digital data for processing and analysis.
- **Operational AI** – AI systems that are actively deployed in business operations to improve efficiency, decision-making, and customer interactions.

P

- **Personalization AI** – AI-driven technology that tailors content, recommendations, and user experiences based on individual preferences and behavior.
- **Predictive Analytics** – The use of AI and data science to analyze historical data and predict future trends, customer behavior, or business outcomes.
- **Prompt Engineering** – The art of designing effective prompts to interact with AI language models, improving the quality of responses and generated content.

Q

- **Quantum AI** – An emerging field that combines quantum computing with AI to solve complex problems at unprecedented speeds.

R

- **Reinforcement Learning** – A type of machine learning

where AI learns by trial and error, receiving rewards or penalties based on its actions.

- **Responsible AI** – AI development and deployment practices that prioritize fairness, transparency, accountability, and ethical considerations.
- **Robotic Process Automation (RPA)** – The use of software robots to automate repetitive business tasks, such as data entry and invoice processing.

S

- **Supervised Learning** – A type of machine learning where AI models are trained on labeled data to make accurate predictions.
- **Synthetic Data** – Artificially generated data used to train AI models when real-world data is scarce or sensitive.

T

- **Turing Test** – A test proposed by Alan Turing to determine whether a machine can exhibit human-like intelligence by engaging in natural conversations.
- **Transfer Learning** – A technique in AI where a pre-trained model is adapted for a new but related task, improving efficiency and accuracy.

U

- **Unsupervised Learning** – A type of machine learning where AI models identify patterns and structures in data without predefined labels.
- **User-Centric AI** – AI designed with a strong focus on

enhancing user experience, personalization, and human interaction.

V

- **Virtual Assistant** – AI-powered software, such as Siri, Google Assistant, and Alexa, that assists users with tasks, answers queries, and provides recommendations.
- **Voice Recognition** – AI technology that converts spoken language into text, enabling applications like speech-to-text and voice assistants.

W

- **Weak AI (Narrow AI)** – AI systems that are designed for specific tasks and lack general intelligence, such as chatbots, recommendation engines, and self-driving cars.
- **Workflow Automation** – The use of AI and automation tools to streamline business processes and reduce manual effort.

X, Y, Z

- **Explainable AI (XAI)** – AI systems designed to provide clear explanations for their decisions, increasing transparency and trust.
- **Zero-Shot Learning** – An AI capability where a model can perform tasks it has never explicitly been trained on by leveraging prior knowledge.